CHILDREN'S LEARNING IN EARLY CHILDHOOD

For my parents

The potential for learning in every child is enormous

CHILDREN'S LEARNING IN EARLY CHILDHOOD

Learning Theories in Practice 0–7 Years

SEAN MACBLAIN

Los Angeles | London | New Delhi
Singapore | Washington DC | Melbourne

Los Angeles | London | New Delhi
Singapore | Washington DC | Melbourne

SAGE Publications Ltd
1 Oliver's Yard
55 City Road
London EC1Y 1SP

SAGE Publications Inc.
2455 Teller Road
Thousand Oaks, California 91320

SAGE Publications India Pvt Ltd
B 1/I 1 Mohan Cooperative Industrial Area
Mathura Road
New Delhi 110 044

SAGE Publications Asia-Pacific Pte Ltd
3 Church Street
#10-04 Samsung Hub
Singapore 049483

Editor: Jude Bowen
Senior assistant editor: Catriona McMullen
Production editor: Katherine Haw
Copyeditor: Tom Bedford
Proofreader: Brian McDowell
Indexer: Charmian Parkin
Marketing manager: Lorna Patkai
Cover design: Wendy Scott
Typeset by: C&M Digitals (P) Ltd, Chennai, India
Printed in the UK

© Sean MacBlain 2021

First published 2021

Apart from any fair dealing for the purposes of research, private study, or criticism or review, as permitted under the Copyright, Designs and Patents Act, 1988, this publication may not be reproduced, stored or transmitted in any form, or by any means, without the prior permission in writing of the publisher, or in the case of reprographic reproduction, in accordance with the terms of licences issued by the Copyright Licensing Agency. Enquiries concerning reproduction outside those terms should be sent to the publisher.

Library of Congress Control Number: 2020950725

British Library Cataloguing in Publication data

A catalogue record for this book is available from the British Library.

ISBN 978-1-5297-1626-9
ISBN 978-1-5297-1625-2 (pbk)

At SAGE we take sustainability seriously. Most of our products are printed in the UK using responsibly sourced papers and boards. When we print overseas we ensure sustainable papers are used as measured by the PREPS grading system. We undertake an annual audit to monitor our sustainability.

CONTENTS

ABOUT THE AUTHOR ix
FOREWORD (BY GLENDA WALSH) xi
ACKNOWLEDGEMENTS xv

INTRODUCTION 1
Aims of the Book 1
About this Book 1
Understanding Learning 2
The Importance of Theory 3
Developmental Readiness 4

PART ONE: THE EARLY PIONEERS 7

1 RECOGNISING THE CONCEPT OF CHILD 9
The Emergence of Childhood 10
   John Locke 11
   Jean-Jacques Rousseau 11
Seeing Nature in Children's Learning 12
   Johann Pestalozzi 12
Valuing Emotional Growth in Early Learning 13
   Sigmund Freud and the Psychodynamic Tradition 13
Recognising the Value of Play in Early Learning 13
   Friedrich Froebel 14
The Need for Social Reform 15
   Rachel and Margaret McMillan 15
Advancing Understanding in Intellectual Development 16
   Rudolf Steiner 16
   Maria Montessori 17

John Dewey and Progressive Education	17
The Emergence of Behaviourism	19

PART TWO: MODERN PERSPECTIVES — 23

2 EMOTIONAL LEARNING IN CHILDHOOD — 25

What Does Emotional Learning Look Like?	26
Sigmund Freud	27
Susan Isaacs	28
Erik Erikson	28
Emotional Intelligence	29
Peter Salovey and John Mayer	30
Daniel Goleman	31
Self-Efficacy	31
Albert Bandura	32
Attachment	34
John Bowlby	34
Michael Rutter	37
Rudolf Schaffer and Peggy Emerson	37

3 SOCIAL LEARNING IN CHILDHOOD — 41

What Does Social Learning Look Like?	42
Poverty and its Impact on Social Learning	43
Bandura and Social Learning	45
Vygotsky and Social Learning	46
Bronfenbrenner and Social Learning	48
Rogoff and Social Learning	49
Gopnik and Social Learning	50
Language and Social Learning	51
Chomsky and the Behaviourist Tradition	52
Vygotsky and Social Language	53
The Ethics of Care	55
Nel Noddings	55
Behaviourism and its Relevance for Social Learning Today	56
Behaviour Modification and Operant Conditioning	56

4 COGNITIVE DEVELOPMENT AND LEARNING — 59

Intellectual Development	60
Piaget	60
Vygotsky	62

Bruner	62
Gardner	63
Freire	64
Play as a Pedagogic Approach	66
Pramling Samuelsson	67
Nutbrown	68
Viewing Learning from the Child's Perspective	69
Moyles	69
Learning: Can We Really Make it Happen Out of Doors?	70
Bilton	70

5 PRACTICE OUTSIDE OF THE MAINSTREAM — 73

Loris Malaguzzi and Reggio Emilia	74
Te Whāriki	75
Sure Start	77
Instrumental Enrichment	78
Challenging Artificial Barriers	78
Assessing Learning	79
The Contribution of Neuroscience	80
Brain Development and Learning in Early Childhood	80
Digital Learning in Early Childhood	81
Digital Challenges in the 21st Century	81

PART THREE: SEEING THEORY IN PRACTICE — 85

6 PLAY AS A PEDAGOGIC APPROACH — 87

Case Study 6.1: Play as Pedagogy: Learning Out of Doors	88

7 EMOTIONAL LEARNING IN EARLY CHILDHOOD — 95

Case Study 7.1: Life Begins for Robbie, Pradeep, and Gita	96
Case Study 7.2: Promoting Self-Efficacy	100

8 SOCIAL LEARNING IN EARLY CHILDHOOD — 105

Case Study 8.1: Robbie, Pradeep, and Gita Start Nursery	106
Case Study 8.2: Giving Meaning to Assessments	110

9 LANGUAGE AND LEARNING — 117

Case Study 9.1: Robbie, Pradeep, and Gita Start School	118
Case Study 9.2: Asperger's Syndrome	124

10 HEALTH AND WELLBEING — 129
Case Study 10.1: Robbie, Pradeep, and Gita Prepare for Key Stage 2 — 130
Case Study 10.2: Wellbeing and Obesity — 138

SOME CONCLUDING THOUGHTS — 143
REFERENCES — 145
INDEX — 151

ABOUT THE AUTHOR

Professor Sean MacBlain PhD is an internationally recognised author whose publications include: MacBlain (Sage, 2020), *Child Development for Teachers*; MacBlain (Sage, 2018), *Learning Theories for Early Years Practice*, now going into its 2nd edition; MacBlain, Dunn and Luke (Sage, 2017), *Contemporary Childhood*; MacBlain, Long and Dunn (Sage, 2015), *Dyslexia, Literacy and Inclusion: Child-Centred Perspectives*; Gray and MacBlain (Sage, 2015), *Learning Theories in Childhood* (2nd edn); MacBlain (Sage, 2014), *How Children Learn*. Sean's publications are used by students, practitioners and academics throughout the world and have been widely translated, including into Chinese and Vietnamese. Sean worked previously at the University of St Mark & St John, Plymouth, England where he held the positions of Research Lead for the Centre for Professional and Educational Research, Research Coordinator for the School of Education, Deputy Chair of the Ethics Committee and member of the Academic Board. Sean has also worked as a Senior Lecturer in Education and Developmental Psychology at Stranmillis University College, Queen's University Belfast and prior to that taught in primary and secondary schools and in Further Education, and as a specialist dyslexia tutor at Millfield independent school. Sean has also worked for over 20 years as an Educational Psychologist. He is married to Angela and lives in Somerset, England.

FOREWORD

This book draws on a wealth of theoretical underpinnings, both historical and modern in approach, to expose a refreshing perspective on children's learning that is multifaceted, holistic and expansive in nature, where the learning needs of the child are perceived as integral to the learning process. Unfortunately, in recent times across Western society, we have become more accustomed to the relentless narrative on accountability and attainment targets, heavily informed by an assessment-led, standards-based and data-driven agenda. In this way, the emphasis on young children's learning has become much reduced and restricted in focus where their social, emotional, cognitive, dispositional and physical needs developed through the medium of play have been relegated to minor status, being deemed less important than academic achievement (Brown and Vaughan, 2009; Walsh, 2019). Such a narrow perspective on children's learning has been exacerbated with the recent lockdown crisis due to the Covid-19 pandemic where a catch-up curriculum, in an effort to redress the period of time learners have experienced outside the normal classroom/setting, has become the new rhetoric, and the potential for an even greater focus to be placed on the core skills of Literacy and Numeracy at the expense of richness and breadth in children's learning is a huge concern (Walsh and Gillespie, 2020).

In this way *Children's Learning in Early Childhood* is particularly timely, as more then ever it is imperative that both students and practising Early Years professionals/teachers are clearly reminded of how young children learn best, along with the underpinning theories that inform such thinking, to ensure that a broad and balanced programme of learning is prioritised which meets the learning needs and interests of each individual child. For too long, Early Years teachers/professionals have clung to an image of theory 'as incomprehensible jargon' (Higgs, 2013: 105), which they deem has little to do with the everyday challenges of the classroom/setting. Yet, in the interests of best practice in Early Years education, the time is ripe to make those who work in the field of Early Years education more 'theoretically astute' (Higgs, 2013: 105) and, in so doing, 'emancipate them from their dependency on practices that are the product of ideological and political agendas' (Higgs, 2013: 105), and I believe that there is no better way to do so than by introducing them to *Children's Learning in Early Childhood*.

Structured into three distinct sections, the author in Part One presents the reader with a series of theoretical lessons from the past and, in so doing, enriches the reader's understanding of those central tenets of Early Years pedagogy which must continue to be prioritised in the Early Years settings today, such as the emergence of childhood, seeing nature in children's learning, valuing emotional growth in early learning and recognising the value of play as learning in practice. Yet to frame such conceptual underpinnings of children's learning solely in an historical context is not the intention of this author. In Part Two, the reader is introduced to a trajectory of more modern theoretical influences with a particular focus on the emotional, social and cognitive aspects of children's learning. These chapters go some way in extending the reader's knowledge and understanding of those fundamentals of Early Years practice presented in Part One, while encouraging a deeper exploration and elaboration on how children's learning potential can be fully nurtured in practice. The author makes no excuse in exposing the complexities of children's learning even further and, as the author argues: 'Taking time to consider and reflect on how others have approached learning in early childhood can be extremely valuable and can impact hugely on one's own practice'.

What makes this book stand out from the rest is the emphasis it places on the effective application of theory into practice. Although the importance of Early Years educators engaging more fully with the theoretical evidence base goes without saying, many student and practising teachers frequently express their concerns about feeling ill-equipped in how they might translate such conceptual understandings into classroom practice, and once again the author of this book has thought ahead. In Part Three of *Children's Learning in Early Childhood*, he brings the content of the whole book to life with nine real case study examples, powerful practices that unite the theory with the practice, links to which are referred to throughout the book. Indeed, the author has gone to great lengths to illustrate the theoretical narrative with further practical examples in the form of hyperlinks to video snapshots, webpage materials, academic articles, discussion points and photographic evidence. In this way the book, as it clearly states in the title, is not simply a narrative of learning theories – instead, such theoretical justifications are clearly contextualised within everyday practice.

In summary, this is certainly a comprehensive and thought-provoking narrative, which provides a rich analysis of past and present learning theories with a direct focus on children aged 0–7 years. But, in my opinion, it does so much more. It certainly brings to our attention the complex nature of young children's learning and clearly illustrates that the nurturing of such learning is anything but straightforward. Furthermore, it clearly showcases that it is only through a thorough interrogation of robust theoretical justifications and rigorous conceptual understandings that sophisticated choices and informed decisions about suitable pedagogies in the Early Years can be appropriately made. Early Years Education is in itself a unique discipline, and those who work in the field must not feel compelled to follow an agenda that has been sketched out with older children in mind. Instead they must have the professional confidence and competence to advocate for all that they know to be fundamental to the high-quality experience that is the right of every young learner, and such a repertoire of knowledge and understanding is deeply embedded in the theories of learning presented in this book. For this reason, I would argue strongly that *Children's Learning in Early Childhood* is a must-read for all those interested in working in the field of early childhood education.

Dr Glenda Walsh, Principal Lecturer and Head of Early Years Education, Stranmillis University College, Belfast

ACKNOWLEDGEMENTS

I would like to offer my sincere thanks to Jude Bowen, who from the outset provided a most valuable and critical sounding board – thank you Jude; my thanks must also go to Catriona McMullen, whose help throughout the editorial stage has been invaluable, and to Katherine Haw and those other colleagues at SAGE who so skilfully guided this text through to final production. I must also pay tribute to my children's children, whose learning I have observed and enjoyed whilst writing this text and who have inspired me daily, and to my good friend Barbara Hendon, a specialist in Early Years who has been so willing to share her considerable expertise. Finally, I wish to thank my wife Angela for her continued love and support throughout.

INTRODUCTION

Aims of the Book

The primary aim of this text is to to support students and early career professionals in the field of Early Years and Primary teaching with demonstrating and applying their knowledge and understanding of early childhood, which is taken to be 0 to 7 years of age. The text will also go a long way in supporting students and trainees with demonstrating how they can apply theory in practice. Over many years working across a range of higher education institutions I (the author) have found that students and trainees preparing to work with young children can often appear confused and even daunted by the wide range of theoretical approaches they encounter. Having also worked as an Educational Psychologist for over 30 years I have found that many Early Years practitioners and teachers can feel very uncertain when asked to articulate their perceptions of children's learning in ways that have a strong basis in theory. This book has been written at a time of monumental change, when children's learning in early childhood is being impacted upon in ways that we have yet to understand by the Coronavirus (COVID-19) pandemic.

About this Book

This book is divided into three parts, with the importance of play as a pedagogical approach in children's learning being a constant thread that runs throughout the text. Part One examines the legacies left to us by the giants in the field of children's learning, and does so by embracing the following themes: the concept of 'child', including the emergence of childhood; the recognition that nature is important in early learning; the value of emotional growth for early learning; the value of play; the need for social reform and how key legacies have informed our understanding of intellectual development. In Part Two, Chapters 2 and 3 explore theoretical approaches to emotional and social learning in childhood, respectively. Chapter 4 then examines cognitive development and learning and introduces the reader to the theoretical perspectives of Piaget, Vygotsky, Bruner, Gardner, and Freire. The importance of seeing play as a pedagogic approach is also explored, with emphasis given to important contributions made by Pramling Samuelsson and Cathy Nutbrown. Viewing learning from the child's perspective is also addressed through the ideas of Janet Moyles, as is learning out of doors with a focus on the work of Helen Bilton. Chapter 5 then explores the insights that can be gained from looking outside of traditional mainstream practice. Themes introduced in Part One and Part Two are picked up in Part Three, in Chapters 6 to 10, and are explored by applying theoretical approaches to nine case studies. We begin, however, by focusing on what is meant by the term 'learning'.

Understanding Learning

Learning is not simply the act of acquiring new information and knowledge; the concept of learning is far more complex (MacBlain, 2014). Indeed, Jarvis (2005) has emphasised the complexity of the concept of learning: '…when we pause and try to define learning in depth, we cannot help but be struck by the awesome breadth and complexity of the concept… What should be the focus of learning, facts or skills?' (pp. 2–3). A further challenge for students being asked to understand and explain learning in childhood is that a great deal of the research in this area has been undertaken within the discipline of psychology, which as Jarvis (2005: 3) has noted:

> …is not a unified body of knowledge and understanding but instead depends on a number of alternative theoretical perspectives or paradigms. Each psychological paradigm has the potential to offer a different vision of the nature of the learner… (p. 3)

Importantly, Smith et al. (2003) have stressed the importance of the environments in which children grow up when they emphasised how learning '…refers to the influence of specific environmental information on behaviour…' (p. 34). A most useful entry point for understanding and explaining learning in early childhood was offered some years previously by Fontana (1995), who suggested using 'descriptions' to explain learning and emphasised how learning '…is not something that happens to individuals… but something which they themselves make happen by the manner in which they handle incoming information and put it to use' (p. 145). Readers may wish to pause and reflect on the specific types of environmental information that have been shaping and defining the communities and societies that children are now growing up in because of the COVID-19 pandemic, and the challenges faced by children in acting upon their environments.

The joy of learning begins early

The Importance of Theory

I (the author) have observed over many years the difficulties that students training to work in the fields of early childhood and teaching have had when trying to deconstruct their own ideas on learning, and perhaps more particularly when asked to apply theory to the experiences they have had when on placements in their written assignments. Walsh (2018) recently highlighted the importance of students and trainees understanding theory when she commented on how '…we need to look at notable philosophies and theorists to help us unravel and deconstruct our own understandings…'. Indeed, Walsh went further, citing McMillan (2009) who emphasised how:

> …an ability to reflect on appropriate theories is essential to equip students to become competent professionals… Failing to embrace these theoretical issues may result in what could be described as narrow and shallow perceptions of what constitutes high quality practice…, which Walsh (2017) suggests will do little to address the real learning needs and interests of the young child. (p. 8)

Responding to the challenges of explaining learning and development through different theoretical positions, Rose and Wood (2016) have advised us to take a 'consilience' approach which 'attempts to draw together different perspectives' (p. 100); indeed, this makes enormous sense. Having a sound understanding of different theoretical approaches helps us with deconstructing our own perceptions of children's learning and, perhaps more importantly, helps when explaining these perceptions to colleagues, other professionals, and parents, or recording them in written form.

Developmental Readiness

Children develop at different rates, and whilst we can observe patterns of learning in young children that appear to be similar, it should be understood that no two children learn in the same way. With physical growth comes sensory development, as in the maturity of visual and auditory capacities, which are important for later learning such as for phonics and the acquisition of literacy and numeracy. Some children may have difficulties with hearing, which can affect their abilities with phonological processing, thereby causing problems with some aspects of spelling and decoding. Others may have visual difficulties, which could cause problems later when they experience difficulties tracking words across a page when reading, thereby delaying their acquisition of literacy and resulting in their falling behind their peers. Though milestones in early childhood prior to entering primary school are explored in successive chapters, it is worth indicating some of the key factors that can be observed in children as they enter the Reception year.

Children entering primary school in their Reception year at five years of age are typically more coordinated and have better precision with many physical actions including balance. They are now losing fatty tissue and building muscle capacity, and some will display growth spurts; most will be able to dress and wash themselves and use the toilet independently. Typically, they will be able to hop and skip, and have the ability to run well and touch their toes without bending their knees. At this age they are learning to ride bicycles without stabilisers and use skipping ropes. Their understanding of rules needed for participation in games such as rounders and football, however, will be limited and beyond some children. They will still be learning to use cutlery with dexterity, cut up their food, use manners appropriately and take their turn when engaged with other children in games and activities. Fine motor skills are developing, and they will be learning to count and exert better control when using a pencil or crayon, completing jigsaw puzzles or when threading beads on a string. They can draw a picture of a person with legs, eyes, mouth, and nose.

Practice in the Reception year has, however, come under some criticism. In January 2017, Her Majesty's Chief Inspector (HMCI) commissioned an Ofsted-wide review of the curriculum (Ofsted, 2017), which focused on the Reception year and the degree to which a school's curriculum for four and five year-olds was preparing them for later formal learning. The review emphasised that the Reception year should be viewed as having 'a unique and important position in education' and as marking a significant milestone in the lives of children. The review stressed how, 'For parents, it is the end of early education and care... and the start of school' (Ofsted, 2017: 8), but also offered the following rather worrying finding:

> For too many children, the Reception year is far from successful. It is a false start and may predispose them to years of catching up rather than forging ahead. In 2016, around one third of children did not have the essential knowledge and understanding they needed to reach a good level of development.

The review went on to offer the following explanation of a 'good' level of development:

> A child achieves a good level of development, as defined by the government, if she or he meets the expected level in the early learning goals in the prime areas of learning (personal, social and emotional development; physical development; and communication and language) and in the specific areas of literacy and mathematics by the age of five.

As children leave the Reception year and move into Year 1, some will be showing natural abilities with some sports as with precision in throwing and catching balls, running, and jumping. Many can skip in time to music, jump off apparatus and ride two-wheeled bicycles without stabilisers, and most will have boundless energy, and will be losing more of their fatty tissue and developing more muscle. Coordination is now becoming more refined, which will be observed in their ability to play group games and games requiring greater skill. They will have developed their drawing skills and use of scissors and paint brushes and will be able to hold pencils and be able to write their first name and surname.

As they move into Year 2, children's motor skills will have now developed much further, and children will be able to achieve greater accuracy when attempting activities that require greater dexterity. They will throw and catch a ball using only one hand and will have greater stamina when running and swimming. They may be more competitive, will have better fine motor skills and will be able to draw pictures of people which have greater detail such as fingers, toes, and clothes. Skills with writing will be much more advanced, and they will be able to write individual letters accurately with sharper differences between upper- and lower-case letters.

PART ONE

THE EARLY PIONEERS

1: Recognising the Concept of Child

In earlier times, such as those of John Locke and Jean-Jacques Rousseau, childhood was not viewed as a distinct stage of development; children were instead seen as 'adults-in-waiting'. With the growth of industrialisation in the UK and the employment of children in factories, new legislation was needed to prevent their exploitation. It remains the case, however, that across the globe large numbers of children continue to be exploited as cheap labour. A report by the International Labour Organisation in 2015 noted, for example, how around 168 million children across the globe were trapped in child labour, which accounted for almost 11 per cent of the overall child population. Many children continue to be exposed to types of labour that cause irreversible physical and mental damage, and even risks to their life, and that impact hugely on their learning and cognitive development.

Whilst the popularised notion of 'childhood' as a time of freedom and fun is widely accepted, it remains the case that for many what it means to be a 'child'—and therefore what it means to learn in childhood—is sadly very different (MacBlain et al., 2017). This is not a recent phenomenon; the challenges in understanding and recognising what it means to be a child have been acknowledged for generations, as evidenced centuries ago when the celebrated philosopher Jean-Jacques Rousseau proposed that 'Childhood is unknown. Starting from the false idea one has of it, the further one goes, the more one loses one's way...' (Rousseau, 1762/1911). It is with this in mind that the first chapter of this text explores what it means to be a 'child'. Part One now looks at the contributions made by a number of key figures over previous generations who challenged the thinking of their times and who brought about significant and positive change for children and their learning, much of which remains relevant even today.

1

RECOGNISING THE CONCEPT OF CHILD

By the end of this chapter you should:

- know why it is important to articulate what it means to be a 'child'
- understand how successive philosophers, theorists and educators have contributed to our knowledge of children's learning and how this continues to inform practice today
- be clear about the value that early pioneers and theorists gave to play as a pedagogy
- fully embrace the importance of viewing learning in early childhood as a unique and individual process in each child

Adults create the experiences that build every young child's view of the world

The Emergence of Childhood

The concept of 'child' has not always been well understood, and children in past centuries were all too often forced to endure conditions and expectations of them that were born largely out of ignorance and a gross lack of understanding of their emotional, social and intellectual development. Sadly, it remains the case that the concept of what it means to be a child is poorly understood in many parts of the world, and across the globe countless numbers of young children continue to endure harsh and uncompromising conditions that would have been more familiar to children living in past centuries in the UK. Just over a decade ago, Hicks (2004) drew attention to the need for all of us to acknowledge the increasingly global context within which children now grow up, a view that has been so starkly accentuated by the recent and devastating COVID-19 pandemic:

> We can only understand life today in our own communities if it is set in the wider global context. What happens elsewhere in the world constantly impacts on our daily lives even if we have not been aware of it… (p. 19)

Fortunately, there have been those in past generations who, in challenging the thinking of their time, have left us with a legacy that has at its core a strong sense of valuing what it means to be a 'child'.

John Locke (1632–1704)

Locke emphasised the importance of seeing childhood as that most special time in the lives of individuals; children, he pronounced, should not be 'hindered' from being children. This was indeed a radical view when one considers that at the time the very idea of childhood as a distinct stage in the lives of young people was given little if any thought by most adults, and the majority of children received little if any formal learning. Locke understood the importance of adults refraining from exercising too much control over learning in childhood, which he believed 'should not be a burden' and should not 'be imposed… with tasks that might become 'irksome' and 'inhibit learning' (MacBlain, 2018a: 13). Locke believed that as children grow, they need to apply reason to how they understand and interpret their worlds and, significantly, that they learn to question what they are told. This was important given the levels of superstition that existed at the time. Locke suggested that children begin life as if they were a 'blank slate', sometimes referred to as *tabula rasa*, and it is on this blank slate that all their experiences, which are gained through the senses, are written.

A key aspect of Locke's approach that continues to define thinking and practice even today was that of *empiricism*. Central to *empiricism* is the notion of 'empirical thinking', which lies very much at the heart of the 'sciences' whereby phenomena are observed from which data are gathered and then quantified. It was this approach that came to underpin the *behaviourist* tradition, offering them a methodology, key to which was the observation, recording and measurement of behaviours, and therefore learning (Gross, 1992; Smith et al., 2003). It needs to be recognised that the *empiricist* view of children's learning is different to that of the *nativist* view where it is argued children inherit their abilities. In the decades that followed John Locke, the celebrated pioneer Rousseau developed the concept of what it means to be a child and how learning in childhood needed to be understood as being different.

Jean-Jacques Rousseau (1712–1778)

Like Locke, Rousseau embraced the concept of 'child' and saw the importance of emotional and social development for children's learning; he was in this respect ahead of his time. Rousseau presented his ideas on children's education in a much-celebrated book, *Emile* (1762/1911), in which he introduced his readers to the life events of a boy named Emile as he progresses through infancy and childhood, and into adulthood. A dominant feature in the thinking of Rousseau's time was that children were born with 'original sin', and that a primary function of education was to purge children of this sin and the associated guilt that came with it. It was also popularly believed that children were born with impulses, which if not addressed would lead to 'wickedness'. Rousseau, in contrast, proposed that all children were born 'good' and, importantly, that what they inherit at birth is what makes up most of their individual potential. He believed a key purpose of education to be the channelling of these impulses in a positive direction, thereby giving children a clearer sense of purpose. He also recognised that society played a substantial role in influencing learning, and that it could be a potential cause for harm as well as good. Children's education, he proposed, should follow the natural growth of the child and pass through stages, the first being from birth to 12 when they are influenced predominantly by impulses, and the second being up to the age of 16, when reason takes over. He saw the role of the tutor as central to developing positive and meaningful environments for learning, as it was through this process that children would come to understand the worlds in which they lived, gain respect for themselves and others, and learn the consequences of their actions, the difference between right and wrong, and honesty and humility.

Seeing Nature in Children's Learning
Johann Pestalozzi (1746–1827)

Today, we take for granted the place of nature in early learning, but this was not always so. Sadly, it remains the case that too many children across the world grow up in urbanised environments where the natural world plays little if any part in their education. Like Locke and Rousseau, Pestalozzi recognised the concept of 'child' and saw nature as a key element in the learning of young children; this is illustrated in his belief that the primary aim of education was that of developing the *head*, the *heart* and the *hands*. Pestalozzi's ideas on learning and the importance of nature in childhood were captured some decades ago in the following quotation, cited by Silber (1965): 'I wish to wrest education from the outworn order of doddering old teaching hacks… and entrust it to the eternal powers of nature herself' (p. 134). Pestalozzi believed that children's early learning should involve active engagement in activities and the use of objects that were part of their natural environment and, like Locke, he believed

Early childhood is a time of wonder

children should be free to follow their own interests. Importantly, he was one of the first pioneers to view teaching as a subject that should be studied in its own right, and because of this he is often referred to as the 'father of pedagogy'. It can be said that Pestalozzi's ideas on children's learning were ahead of their time, for he believed that children need to learn by engaging with the world around them through their actions and within their environments, and being encouraged by adults to pursue their own interests.

Valuing Emotional Growth in Early Learning

Sigmund Freud (1856–1939) and the Psychodynamic Tradition

Locke, Rousseau and Pestalozzi all understood the importance of recognising what it is to be a child and how emotions impact significantly on learning in early childhood. Later, towards the end of the 19th century, a major shift in thinking began to emerge as philosophers and theorists wrestled with the emerging discipline of psychology; this shift accelerated with the emergence of *psychodynamics* and most notably the work of Freud, who placed enormous emphasis on what it means to be a child and how experiences in early childhood affect later development and learning. In his original work Freud proposed that at the core of individual development are two determining elements, characterised by pleasure and by tensions; tensions, he suggested, arise from sexual energy (the libido), with pleasure emanating from a release of this sexual energy. It should be emphasised that Freud used the term 'sexual' in a broad sense to account for thoughts and actions that individuals find pleasurable. Freud also proposed that children and young people move through a series of stages: *Oral, Anal, Phallic, Latency* and *Genital*, with the first of these following birth. His ideas were then developed by others and applied specifically to learning in early childhood, most notably perhaps by Susan Isaacs (discussed later in Chapter 2).

Chapter Link

The ideas of Freud and Isaacs are explored in greater detail in Chapter 2.

Recognising the Value of Play in Early Learning

Whilst the early pioneers saw the value of play in early childhood and how play was central to learning, they were largely isolated in their thinking from popular practice. It must be remembered that learning in previous generations was for the most part formal and highly prescriptive, and at times brutal, as indicated by the historian Ruth Goodman who wrote about children's education in the Victorian era, as follows:

Many teachers firmly believed that an error in a child's work was the result of 'not trying', of the child not having listened properly to their instruction. Child after child was beaten for their spelling mistakes, grammatical errors, incorrect sums and messy handwriting. (Goodman, 2013: 292)

One pioneer, however, whose ideas focused on the value of play in children's learning, and who drew heavily on the ideas of Locke, Rousseau, and Pestalozzi, was Froebel.

Friedrich Froebel (1782–1852)

Froebel (1887) was one of the first pioneers to fully embrace play as central to children's learning and their emotional and social development. Froebel saw the value of play in supporting children's learning and, more particularly, how play could advance and extend thinking and learning. He believed, for example, that children could express their individual nature through play, and it was this idea that lay very much at the heart of his philosophy of learning. Froebel's significant and enlightened contribution to our understanding of the importance of play in children's learning was expressed most eloquently by Tizard and Hughes (1984: 4), who drew attention to how the kindergarten and nursery school begun by Froebel had 'freed' young children from the harsh and overly prescriptive learning of their time, when children were typically made to sit passively, be drilled by their teachers, and subjected largely to memorising and rote learning.

In developing his ideas on the value of play in learning, Froebel developed an array of educational materials which he believed could support and extend learning in children. These materials, or 'gifts' as he called them, included such items as objects of different shapes that could be employed by teachers to stimulate children's thinking and learning, for example: Gift 1: Small soft balls knitted or made of rubber with three being in the primary colours, red, yellow and blue, and the other in the secondary colours of green, orange and purple. Gift 2: A box in which was contained a wooden cylinder, a cube, and a sphere with holes. Gift 3: A box with eight one-inch cubes made of wood. Gift 4: New shapes of varying sizes and dimensions. Gift 5: A box, different in size to others with blocks of a different size and of a greater number (see the following link for further information on Froebel's gifts: www.froebel.org.uk/training-and-resources/froebels-gifts).

Froebel promoted the idea of children being active and learning through engagement with tasks that have purpose and that are meaningful to them. He also promoted the idea of children being active out of doors and, like Pestalozzi, emphasised the importance of children learning from and through nature.

Case Study Link

The benefits of learning through nature are explored further in Chapter 6, Case Study 6.1.

Froebel believed strongly in the potential of music to support and extend children's learning, particularly singing, which he believed was a feature of children's play. Froebel's ideas were in many respects ahead of their time and continue to influence thinking and practice even today. Miller and Pound (2011) have, for example, noted how those who promoted Froebel's ideas in past years have been influencing official policy from as far back as the Hadow Report published in 1931 and, importantly, how there has been a recent trend in Froebel training in the UK where '…the next generation of Froebelians is emerging, trained in the practical apprenticeship way, in reflective practice through in-service training' (p. 64).

The Need for Social Reform

Central to the emerging concept of what it meant to be a child in past generations was the importance of embracing social reform. Two early pioneers who challenged the thinking of their time and who embraced the value of positive learning experiences in early childhood were the McMillan sisters.

Rachel (1859–1917) and Margaret (1860–1931) McMillan

The McMillan sisters confronted many of the social issues of their time and were responsible for improving the health and wellbeing of countless numbers of children, and thereby their learning. In 1904, Margaret published *Education through the Imagination*, and in her later years played an influential role in the training of teachers, going on to found the Rachel McMillan College in 1930 with the aim of improving the training of those wishing to work with young children in her nurseries. Like Margaret, Rachel believed that involving children in caring for animals and plants was an important means of developing within them the values of caring, not only for themselves but also for others.

Being a Child in the 19th Century

The challenges facing Rachel and Margaret were considerable: at the time, the concept of 'child' was little understood and not given anything like the attention it is today. It was estimated, for example, by Horn (1997) that in the years between 1800 and 1850 there were within the city of London some 30,000 homeless children living on the streets who were uneducated, undernourished and lacking in supervision. Indeed, it was only in 1899 that school attendance was made compulsory and even then, many children failed to attend as they were needed by their parents to work and bring in additional income. Following a sustained campaign, Rachel and Margaret were successful in having free school meals introduced for children, with the passing of the Provision of School Meals Act in 1906. The sisters went on to found what was to become the *Nursery Movement* and brought to public attention the benefits of children having open-air learning, which was in many ways a direct response to the overcrowded and filthy living conditions in which children lived.

Rachel and Margaret were also influential in having the government of the day introduce medical inspections for children in schools, with the first clinic opening its doors in 1908. Between 1831 and 1866 some 150,000 individuals had died of cholera, with life expectancy in London in the 1840s being around 30 to 40 years, turning many children into orphans. In the mid 1800s George Graham (Registrar General) and William Farr, his assistant, noted how in the city of Liverpool that of 100,000 children born a mere 44,797 lived to the age of 20 (Hutchinson, 2017: 95). The need for medical inspections can also be seen in the fact that in 1851 one British person out of every 979 was blind (Hutchinson, 2017: 96–7), which was attributed to smallpox, a virus that was spread through minute droplets from the saliva of an infected person often caused by coughing or close contact. It was only two years later in 1853 that vaccinations against smallpox became compulsory, following an Act of Parliament.

Advancing Understanding in Intellectual Development

Different approaches have emerged over the years that have added much to our understanding of the concept of 'child' and how intellectual development impacts on learning in childhood. We now look at four different approaches that have added to our understanding of what it is to be a 'child' and why high-quality learning in childhood is so important.

Rudolf Steiner (1861–1925)

Steiner saw the purpose of education as responding to the changing needs of children, with particular emphasis on their intellectual and emotional needs. Steiner founded his first school in the city of Stuttgart when invited to do so by a leading industrialist, Waldorf Astoria, the owner of a large cigarette factory who wanted a school to educate the children of his factory workers, and so Steiner schools came to be known as Steiner-Waldorf schools. A key feature of the Steiner-Waldorf tradition was the importance of imitation in children's learning (Miller and Pound, 2011). The nature of the relationships that Steiner practitioners build with their children is also seen as extremely important and central to children's learning. The approach emphasises how up to age seven, play, drawing and art and the natural world are key, with links between science and art also being important.

Before seven, children are not formally taught reading, the rationale being that children will learn to read naturally if they have already developed emotionally and socially. This is also the case in mathematics, with children being introduced to formal learning in mathematics later than children in mainstream state schools. Interestingly, the Steiner philosophy advocates that children are taught to write before being taught to read. Children are also encouraged to sing every day and to learn how to play musical instruments; they create their own lesson books and are encouraged to write and illustrate these. Assessment happens through observation, with a key focus given to emotional and social development. Where possible, children keep the same teacher through primary school, as by doing so it is believed they learn the value of relationships, in addition to benefiting from the knowledge their teacher has accumulated about their emotional and social development. Teachers employ a 'narrative' approach to learning and place a great deal of emphasis on children being encouraged to listen; in this way they are encouraged to build internal representations of the characters in stories, which develops their imagination. Observation plays a significant role in Steiner-Waldorf schools.

Maria Montessori (1870–1952)

Montessori saw the environment as hugely important, and today Montessori teachers continue to place great emphasis on the learning environments they create. Creativity was also seen by Montessori as important, with children being given time and space, which not only supports learning but allows them to flourish. Montessori viewed learning through the senses as being important, in addition to children being taught to take responsibility for their own learning, which includes looking after themselves and their environments. Repetition was also seen as important in children's learning and as a means of enhancing creative thinking and promoting over-learning, which would lead to the internalisation of new concepts and deeper understanding, and, crucially, preparation for later more formal and abstract learning. Central to Montessori's ideas was the notion of 'planes', or 'stages', through which children pass as they grow and develop. During the first plane children progress by taking their first steps and using their first words to engage socially with others around them. Montessori proposed that within this first stage there were eleven 'sensitive' periods: Movement; Language; Small Objects; Order; Music; Grace and Courtesy; Refinement of the Senses; Writing Fascination; Reading; Spatial Relationships; and Mathematics. As children then progress to the next stage they can be observed running and jumping, climbing onto objects and importantly engaging in conversation with others, which is a demonstration of the fact that they can employ quite complex and sophisticated abilities in their use of language. Children are also developing an understanding that others have feelings and are learning to adapt their own behaviours in response to those of others. They are also forming friendships and adapting their behaviours to respond appropriately to the complex nature of social interactions with those they meet outside of the immediate family. Their abilities with memory are also developing in addition to their expressive and receptive language. Montessori also devoted much time to understanding children with learning difficulties and had a great deal of success with children who would have been seen as uneducable.

John Dewey (1859–1952) and Progressive Education

Dewey approached intellectual development in childhood very differently to many of his contemporaries and is often associated with the term 'progressive education' and the notion of 'child-centred education'. At the time of developing his ideas, education was dominated largely by thinking and practice located within the *behaviourist* tradition, discussed later. In challenging the thinking and practice of his time Dewey was seen and is still seen by some to be extremely controversial; the depth of the controversy he provoked with his ideas on intellectual development and learning in schools can be seen in the following quotation by the British philosopher Richard Pring (2007), who commented as follows:

> ...when I came to Oxford in 1989, I was seated at dinner next to Lord Keith Joseph, who had been Secretary of State for Education under Prime Minister Margaret Thatcher. He accused me of being responsible for all the problems in our schools – because I had introduced teachers to John Dewey. (p. 3)

Though Dewey saw structure as important in children's learning he is perhaps more noted for his view that experiences should be central to children's learning. While he maintained that children require direction and support with their learning, he also persisted in his view that educators should take full account of the individuality of each child, which he saw as being both genetic and experiential.

The Laboratory School

Central to Dewey's philosophy of education were his beliefs, derived in large part from his 'Laboratory School', which he had opened in the city of Chicago in 1896 and which admitted children from nursery age through to their 12th grade. It was in this school that Dewey subjected his own ideas about education and learning to scrutiny. Pring (2007) commented that:

> ...behind Dewey's experimental school was a particular view of the normal young learner: someone who is curious and interested, but whose curiosity and interests had been sapped by modes of learning which took no account of that *interest* in learning... (p. 16)

Dewey believed that schools are communities and should be viewed accordingly; he also emphasised the notion that teachers cannot change the experiences children and young people have already had. Drawing once more on Pring (2007) we can gain further insights into Dewey's ideas on learning and children's education, as follows:

> First, the school should be an extension of the home and the community... Second... the school should value manual and practical activity... Third, the interests of young people were to be treated as of importance in their own right... Fourth... Their [school subjects] value lies in their usefulness... Fifth, a young person whose interests are taken seriously and whose teacher seeks to develop those interests... will be disciplined by the pursuit of those interests... (pp. 15–17)

In summary, Dewey proposed that it is what each child draws from their experience that is important and that children experience events in different ways, therefore what is of benefit to one child may not be of benefit to another.

The Emergence of Behaviourism

Whilst John Locke introduced us to the principles of *empiricism*, the *behaviourists* took this idea much further, observing, analysing, measuring and quantifying learning through systematic observation of behaviours. *Behaviourism* is premised on the idea that associations develop between stimuli and responses and that these account for learning.

Is Behaviourism Still Relevant?

Daniels and Shumow (2002) captured what is a key criticism of *behaviourism* and one that has led many theorists to challenge its use in understanding the complexity of children's learning in overly simplistic terms when they emphasised how *behaviourism* 'assumes that children do not develop on their own; rather development consists of learning sets of relatively passive responses to environmental stimuli, such as the teacher' (p. 505). More recently, Papatheodorou and Potts (2016) articulated the key principles of *behaviourism* as follows:

> ...behaviourists saw learning as being the direct outcome of responses to environmental stimuli through a process of (positive and/or negative) reinforcement... the child makes an association between a stimulus and the consequences that follow the triggered behaviour; a rewarding consequence is likely to increase the occurrence of the exhibited behaviour, while a punishing consequence would minimize it. (p. 112)

Papatheodorou and Potts also offered a helpful clarification of the difference between *behaviourism* and the sociocultural theory of Vygotsky, whose approach had also contrasted in many respects with that of Piaget:

> Vygotsky (2002) argued that development and learning take place within the social and cultural milieu: children are neither the lone scientists, isolated from their social environment (assumed in Piaget's theory), nor the product of direct stimuli of the environment and the process of positive or negative reinforcement (argued by behaviourists). Children are the product of their socio-cultural milieu, its beliefs and values, and its customs and practices. (p. 114)

An often-cited quotation which encapsulates the thinking of the early behaviourists was that offered by Watson (1928), who declared:

> Give me a dozen healthy infants, well-formed, and my own specified world to bring them up in and I'll guarantee to take any one at random and train him to become any type of specialist I might select... regardless of his talents, penchants, tendencies, abilities, vocations and the race of his ancestors. (p. 82)

The extent to which *behaviourism* dominated practice has been articulated by Daniels and Shumow (2002: 496–7) as follows:

...actual educational practice throughout this time period has been modelled on conceptions of learning and development defined by the behaviourist tradition (Brown, 1994) or by extreme biological views such as entity ideas that intelligence is fixed or maturationist views that children develop on their own.

Daniels and Shumow went on to emphasise how in recent decades psychologists have 'denounced those prevailing beliefs and practices' that were a legacy of this dominant approach, which meant that 'attention has been refocused on "child-centred" practices, identified with constructivist, social constructivist, or ecological theories' (p. 496). Importantly, they also stress that whilst 'some conceive of the differences among theories as irreconcilable (Case, 1998), others see these as complementing one another (Cobb, 1994)':

Common threads relevant to education among these theorists include the ideas that effective teaching must be based on understanding the child and the vision of children as active agents in their own education. (Daniels and Shumow: 497)

Key principles of *behaviourism* have been challenged by some theorists such as Piaget and Bruner, who saw developmental growth and learning in childhood differently and rejected what they argued was an overly simplistic explanation of learning based on stimuli and responses. Piaget and Bruner, amongst others, looked in greater depth at internal cognitive processes that they argued were at the core of children's thinking. Recently, Gray and MacBlain (2015: 65) revealed the intensity of Piaget's criticism of *behaviourism* (Piaget, 1952) who argued that '...it merely encouraged the repetition of 'meaningless strings' and 'circus tricks' but failed to promote understanding'. Buckler and Castle (2014) have also emphasised how Piaget and Bruner rejected the principles of *behaviourism* and focused more on children's cognitive processing and the internal workings of the brain: 'The cognitive perspective emphasises the importance of explaining behaviour in terms of internal events, the meaning of concepts and processes, beliefs, attitudes and intentions' (p. 18).

They went on to stress how theoretical approaches within the field of *cognitive psychology* had focused more on 'cognitions', for example, 'thoughts, language, memory, decision-making, attention and information processing – that inform our everyday lives' (p. 19), which had been largely ignored by the early *behaviourists*. It should be recognised, however, that whilst more recent cognitive theories have largely superseded and even replaced *behaviourist* approaches, Early Years practitioners and teachers continue to employ the principles of *behaviourism*, though often without being aware they are doing so; they shape children's learning, for example (often unwittingly), through reinforcement, by giving praise and using such tactics as 'star charts' when they want to increase desired behaviours. Though *behaviourism* declined in popularity it has seen something of a revival in more recent years as teachers and practitioners have come to better understand its principles and to recognise that on most days they are in fact employing *behaviourist* principles in their own practice (Wheldall, 2012).

Chapter Summary

- We need to embrace more fully the concept of 'child' and view childhood within a global context.
- Whilst dissimilar, the legacies left to us by early pioneers and theorists have enriched our understanding of what it is to be a child and why pedagogies in childhood need to be of a high quality.
- It is important to recognise that many of the legacies left to us by early pioneers and theorists continue to influence and inform practice today.
- Learning in early childhood should be viewed as a unique and individual process for every child.
- It needs to be more fully recognised that play is central to pedagogy in the Early Years.

Extended Reading

Aubrey, K. and Riley, A. (2019) *Understanding & Using Educational Theories* (2nd edn). London: Sage. A comprehensive text that explores a wide range of theoretical approaches together with insights into how these might be applied within classroom settings.

Edwards, C. (2002) 'Three approaches from Europe: Waldorf, Montessori, and Reggio Emilia', *Early Childhood, Research and Practice*, 4 (1), available at: www.researchgate.net/publication/26390918_Three_Approaches_from_Europe_Waldorf_Montessori_and_Reggio_Emilia (accessed: 3 October 2020). An excellent article that explains in clear and accessible terms the differences between three key approaches to learning in early childhood.

Wyse, D. and Rodgers, S. (2016) *A Guide to Early Years and Primary Teaching*. London: Sage. A comprehensive and accessible text that explores a wide range of issues relevant to practice in Early Years settings and primary schools and is full of useful insights.

PART TWO

MODERN PERSPECTIVES

2: Emotional Learning in Childhood
3: Social Learning in Childhood
4: Cognitive Development and Learning
5: Practice Outside of the Mainstream

Part Two now explores a range of theoretical approaches that have emerged in more recent generations and that influence thinking and practice today. The different theoretical approaches are explored thematically over the next four chapters using the following headings: 'Emotional Learning in Childhood', 'Social Learning in Childhood', 'Cognitive Development and Learning' and 'Practice Outside of the Mainstream'.

2

EMOTIONAL LEARNING IN CHILDHOOD

By the end of this chapter you should:

- appreciate that emotional learning in early childhood is key to future learning and the realisation of potential
- recognise that many young children face significant barriers in their emotional learning, including challenges posed by the COVID-19 pandemic
- understand why good attachment is important in early childhood and how neglect and poor attachment can impact significantly on future learning
- be clear that developing strong self-efficacy in early childhood is crucial for effective learning
- understand why it is important for Early Years practitioners and teachers in primary schools to promote holistic learning in early childhood

Emotional learning has its basis in security and feeling loved

What Does Emotional Learning Look Like?

Key to emotional learning in childhood are approaches that are child-centred and holistic and that place a strong emphasis on children valuing themselves as learners. Recently, Rose and Wood (2016) captured the need for such approaches when they referred to young children's learning as 'a holistic and multi-layered process affected by shifting and interacting multiple layers of influence' (p. 86). The importance of teachers understanding the relationship between emotional learning and the realisation of potential was recently accentuated by Hope (2018), as follows:

> Ultimately, a teacher's responsibility is to nurture her students, by recognizing their potentiality and by not conflating a child's potentiality with ability groups or over-identifying a child with limited labels. (p. 36)

Following birth, children adapt to events in their lives and to the changing environments around them and, as they grow, they need stability and security and, importantly, consistency. How they express their feelings and emotions when first starting primary school will reflect their levels of maturity and will of course vary enormously from one child to the next; something that upsets one child might, for example, excite and motivate another child.

Children born into families where they feel secure and nurtured typically have more positive life experiences than children growing up in dysfunctional families characterised by instability and inconsistency and poor role modelling from parents and primary caregivers.

Case Study Link

This theme is explored later in Chapters 7, 8, 9 and 10, in Case Studies 7.1, 8.1, 9.1 and 10.1, respectively.

The emotional experiences that children have when young can shape much of their future learning. Some years ago, Claxton, author of the report *An Intelligent Look at Emotional Intelligence* (ATL, 2005), commissioned by the Association of Teachers and Lecturers, drew attention to how children even at a very young age engage in an 'emotional apprenticeship' where they observe how others around them manage their emotions: 'When uncertain how to respond emotionally to a new person or event, babies and toddlers take their cue from the facial expression and tone of voice of the people they trust'. Claxton went on to emphasise the importance of adult family members acting as good role models for children's emotional learning as they 'deliberately or inadvertently… steer the child's emotional development…'. Presenting poor role modelling can, he maintained, have poor consequences for children: 'Being around an adult who continually "loses it" is bad for a child's own emotional development' (p. 20). We now explore further the ideas of one celebrated figure referred to in Chapter 1 who offered an important framework for understanding and explaining emotional learning in children.

Sigmund Freud

Freud was a key pioneer in the emergence of psychology and the field of *psychodynamics*, and perhaps most notably, *psychoanalysis*; though open to debate, his ideas have been hugely influential and have made a significant contribution to our attempts at understanding and explaining development and learning in childhood (Miller and Pound, 2011: 22). Freud proposed that at the core of individual development are two determining elements, characterised by 'pleasure' and 'tensions'; he suggested that tensions arise from sexual energy (the libido), with pleasure emanating from a release of this sexual energy (MacBlain, 2018a), and that children move through stages, the first being the *oral* stage from birth to around the end of the first year. During this stage children's personalities are in part being shaped by their libido, and they derive satisfaction from putting things in their mouths, which meets the needs of the libido. This is followed by the *anal* stage from 12 months to around 36 months when the libido is more directed towards the anus and children are becoming aware that their own needs may conflict with those of others, and are experiencing themselves as individuals. Disproportionate insistence during toilet training can also lead to children becoming anally retentive in adulthood. Children then move through the *phallic* stage from around 5 to 6 years of age when the libido is becoming centred around the genitals and they are becoming more aware of the differences between the sexes, which can bring degrees of conflict manifested by physical attraction to others but also rivalries and even jealousy. This is followed by the *latency* stage leading up to puberty when sexual impulses become repressed and sexual energy is redirected towards external activities such as hobbies and friendships. The *genital* stage follows from puberty to adolescence when young people are forming their identities and engaging in experimentation. One notable pioneer who took the original ideas of Freud and adapted these for use in early childhood learning was Susan Isaacs.

Susan Isaacs

Isaacs has brought much to our understanding of how emotions impact on early learning. Born in the Victorian era she would have been aware of the overly strict and harsh experiences that Goodman (2013) referred to in Chapter 1, when children's education was characterised largely by control and punishment. In challenging this type of learning, Isaacs threw herself wholeheartedly into promoting learning in early childhood that embraced the sensitivity and vulnerability of young children. After responding to an advert placed in a newspaper by two individuals who wished to open a school for very young children, Isaacs established the Malting House School, and this gave her the opportunity to implement her ideas on learning, which were based along the principles developed by Freud and his followers. Isaacs believed, for example, that Early Years settings could and should offer the sort of warmth and love that young children ought to receive in their homes, in addition to offering fresh and motivating experiences; in this respect, she saw nursery school as an extension of the home and not as something separate.

Isaacs drew upon her training in psychoanalysis and viewed play as an important means of self-expression, which allowed children to work through difficult feelings and hidden emotions safely and in environments where they could be supported emotionally by adults. She placed great emphasis on the benefits of adults 'getting inside' the worlds that children create but without hindering their natural thinking, by listening patiently to them and observing closely how they behaved and what captured their interest. Despite the attempts made by Isaacs and many of her successors to advocate for proper recognition of the importance of emotional learning in childhood, this has been an area that only in recent years received the attention it deserves (MacBlain et al., 2017; Whitebread, 2012). One other notable figure who developed Freud's original ideas was Erik Erikson.

Erik Erikson

Erikson's *Theory of Psychosocial Development* proposed that individuals move through eight stages during development, with successful progression through each stage leading to balanced and healthy personalities. In contrast, unsuccessful progression through the stages can lead to personalities that lack balance. His theory offers a most useful way of reflecting on and explaining emotional learning in children; the first five stages that reflect development in children are as follows:

Stage 1. *Trust versus Mistrust* (birth to 18 months). During this stage children develop a sense of trust in the world around them and in their primary caregivers. At this stage, trust is largely dependent upon the consistency and reliability of the care they receive. If their care is characterised by a lack of consistency and reliability then they learn to mistrust, which may impact on their future relationships.

Stage 2. *Autonomy versus Shame and Doubt* (2 to 3 years). During this stage children develop independence and autonomy and are learning that they can have choice over what they eat and how they play. Parents play an important part in supporting their children's growth towards independence by providing them with opportunities to achieve success, thereby developing their self-confidence and self-efficacy. Readers might pause here and reflect on how the COVID-19 pandemic is impacting on children at this stage when their parents and Early Years practitioners are having to grapple with the challenges of social distancing, the wearing of masks and the exaggerated control over children's physical environments, not to mention the restrictions placed on children meeting with wider family members such as grandparents.

Stage 3. *Initiative versus Guilt* (3 to 5 years). Language is improving and children are developing their ability to empathise with others and are now asking lots of questions. It is during this stage that children increasingly acquire a sense of purpose. Again, readers might consider here the impact that COVID-19 is having on all children at this stage and the next stages globally.

Stage 4. *Industry versus Inferiority* (6 to 12 years). Learning is now more formal, and teachers and peers have become important role models. Winning approval is important, as, through this, children develop a sense of pride in who they are and in what they can achieve.

Stage 5. *Identity versus Role Confusion* (13–18 years) relates to the years following primary school.

Case Study Link

Erikson's stages are explored further in Chapters 7, 8, 9 and 10, in Case Studies 7.1, 8.1, 9.1 and 10.1, respectively.

Emotional Intelligence

Emotional intelligence impacts significantly on children's emotional learning and cognitive development in early childhood (MacBlain et al., 2017; MacBlain 2020). We know that emotional intelligence requires children to receive guidance not only with recognising and

Children are already developing independence and autonomy from an early age

understanding the emotions of others but, importantly, understanding and managing their own emotions; by doing so, children develop their abilities to engage effectively with others and with new situations as, for example, when entering pre-school and later, primary school. This important developmental process has been explained by Salovey and Mayer (1990) as 'emotional intelligence' sometimes referred to as 'emotional literacy' (Goleman, 1996). Salovey and Mayer (1990) defined emotional intelligence as that 'subset of social intelligence that involves the ability to monitor one's own and others' feelings and emotions, to discriminate among them and to use this information to guide one's thinking and actions' (p. 189). This definition is a helpful one as it emphasises the importance of viewing emotional intelligence as a subset of wider 'social intelligence'.

Peter Salovey and John Mayer

Salovey and Mayer (1990) proposed four key factors central to developing good emotional intelligence, namely: *perceiving, reasoning, understanding,* and *managing* emotions. From birth, children observe and come to understand with increasing accuracy the emotions of those around them, and later others they meet outside of their homes, through being increasingly sensitive to how others behave in different situations and by making interpretations of facial expressions; this is in addition to making interpretations of the body language of others. By doing so, they develop their understanding of what certain behaviour patterns mean and importantly learn about the power of their own spoken language and that of others. Children then engage increasingly with their own emotions with the result that they expand their intellectual functioning and cognitive abilities; they also attach meaning increasingly to emotions they observe, and in doing so learn to manage their own emotions. Here, readers might pause to consider how young children perceive the emotions of adults around them who are responding to COVID-19 and how they might interpret and try to understand the changes around them.

Daniel Goleman

Goleman (1996: 48) has offered a most useful means of exploring children's emotional responses to phenomena, which can help practitioners and teachers explain children's responses to events such as the COVID-19 pandemic. Referring to the original work of Mayer (co-author with Salovey), Goleman drew attention to how Mayer proposed that children fall into distinctive styles of dealing with emotions:

- *Self-aware*, where they grow an awareness of their own feelings as these occur but do not ruminate over these feelings.
- *Engulfed*, where they feel 'swamped' by their emotions and 'helpless' when attempting to overcome them, meaning that they do little then to escape from difficult feelings and emotions where, for example, adults might mistakenly view them as simply being in a bad mood.
- *Accepting*, where they simply accept their feelings without attempting to alter them.

Early Years practitioners and teachers will experience children managing their emotions in these different styles and will be aware of how the different styles impact positively and/or negatively on learning. These styles offer practitioners and teachers a structure which can help when explaining to others the responses they observe in young children who may appear alarmed or fearful of change and events and phenomena that they do not have the cognitive maturity as yet to understand.

Critical Question

What practical steps can Early Years practitioners take to support children who regularly appear to be engulfed by emotions they do not understand?

Self-Efficacy

Even in the hours following birth children are engaging in emotional and social learning, and they do this through their interactions with others around them and with their environments. In the weeks and months following birth their learning will develop at quite an amazing rate and children will gradually develop a sense of who they are and what they are capable of. This process is of course variable as each child will learn differently and encounter events and experience relationships in their childhood that support or, sadly, distort this whole process.

Case Study Link

This process is illustrated further in Chapters 7, 8, 9 and 10, in Case Studies 7.1, 8.1, 9.1 and 10.1, respectively.

Albert Bandura

Some decades ago, Bandura (1977, 1997) sought to explain how learning in childhood is influenced by social interaction, and particularly relationships, in his *Social Learning* theory. In doing so he placed enormous importance on the notion of 'self-efficacy', which he proposed is central to how children perceive their abilities and potential. Recently, Whitebread (2012: 9) drew attention to how subsequent research in this area has underpinned the importance of self-efficacy for learning and educational achievement.

It is now widely accepted (Colverd and Hodgkin, 2011) that children with poor self-efficacy have a strong tendency to avoid activities that present a challenge and typically allow their thinking to be dominated by negative feelings about their abilities. In addition, they typically demonstrate low self-esteem and are reluctant to attempt new challenges and see these through to completion. These children can be observed to display outward signs of anxiety when asked to engage in tasks that require them to problem-solve and that they perceive to be challenging; in this way, they place artificial limitations on what they think they are capable of, and therefore reinforce internal beliefs about their own abilities that lead them to think that activities that present them with a challenge are too often beyond their capabilities, when in fact this is not the case.

Children with poor self-efficacy also struggle to identify personal goals and may demonstrate limited commitment when asked to work in groups with their peers; they may also place overly harsh limits on themselves. Colverd and Hodgkin (2011: 36) have proposed that adults working with these children can observe external behaviours that reflect internal dialogues children are having where they say to themselves, 'I can't do this, it's boring', which in truth signals their real thinking, 'I don't believe I can be successful with this and therefore I don't want to take the risk'. Bandura identified four key psychological processes (Figure 2.1), which he proposed were heavily influenced by the self-efficacy beliefs that individuals have of themselves, namely: 'cognitive', 'motivational', 'affective' and 'selection' (Hayes, 1994: 477):

We know from the theoretical approaches already discussed that self-efficacy cannot be taught; however, there is a great deal that Early Years practitioners and teachers can do to support its development. Bandura proposed a number of factors that can be helpful in this process, one of which is for children to develop a sense of 'mastery' through experiences such as observing other children with high levels of self-efficacy when learning, engaging with and being supported by adults in completing challenges and having regular verbal affirmation from significant adults, and being supported in gaining increased understanding of emotions and feelings as these arise. For many children, however, the level to which they can strengthen self-efficacy will be affected by adverse experiences such as impoverished relationships and emotional neglect by their parents and primary caregivers (Colverd and Hodgkin, 2011; Main and Solomon, 1986).

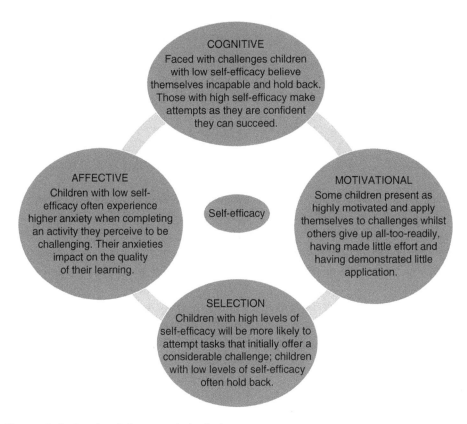

Figure 2.1 Bandura's four psychological processes

Critical Question

What practical steps can Reception class teachers take to improve self-efficacy in children who are withdrawn and who struggle to mix with their peers?

Strong self-efficacy has its foundations in early and loving relationships

Attachment

The benefits of secure attachment and the problems associated with disordered attachment are now well recognised (McKee, 2004). Following birth, children are increasingly separated from their primary caregivers and after initial periods of separation they are then generally comforted. As periods of separation become more frequent, children come to understand that their caregivers will return and they will not be hurt by these temporary absences; in this way, they are prepared for dealing with environments outside of their homes. Two important approaches have emerged which have helped our understanding of attachment: that offered by the *behaviourists* and that which has been called the *evolutionary* approach.

The *behaviourists* proposed that attachment can be explained by learned behaviours; new-born infants need sustenance (milk) in order to survive, hence attachment is first learned through association or the infant's attachment to the person who is providing the milk. The child 'learns' to associate the milk with the comfort it is feeling from the caregiver who is feeding them – this can be understood in the context of 'classical conditioning'. Infants then learn that their own behaviours such as smiling and crying can bring pleasant and comforting responses from adults and that by initiating these behaviours they can receive more responses – this can be understood in terms of *operant conditioning*, which is central to the *behaviourist* approach and is discussed later in Chapter 3.

John Bowlby

The *evolutionary* approach can be located in the work of John Bowlby (1988), who was heavily influenced by the early work of Harlow (1964). In contrast to the *behaviourist* approach,

Bowlby believed that at birth children are already programmed biologically to form attachments, which are necessary for their safety and security. When infants cry, for example, they typically evoke comforting responses from their parents, and in this way, they achieve security. For some children, however, this is not the case, which leads to problems with attachment. Bowlby proposed that infants need to attach to their mothers during the first five years of their lives and that if this fails to happen then children develop a pathology characterised by problems with forming affectionate attachments with others in later life. He further argued that maternal deprivation in early development can result in significant problems during adolescence and cause behavioural problems.

Case Study Link

These issues are explored further in Chapters 7, 8 and 10, in Case Studies 7.1, 8.1, and 10.1, respectively.

In the 1970s and 1980s Mary Ainsworth, a co-researcher with Bowlby, took up his ideas and developed them further. In doing so, she offered a set of classifications which are a useful means of understanding and explaining 'attachment' and 'attachment disorder' in young children, and the effects of these on subsequent emotional, social, and cognitive development.

Focus on Theory: Ainsworth and the Strange Situation

The classifications developed by Ainsworth were, *securely attached; insecurely attached/avoidant*; and *insecurely attached/ambivalent*. In later years, Main and Solomon (1986) added a further classification – *disorganised*. When *securely attached* an infant displays a preference for their primary caregiver, and after being separated from the primary caregiver can be observed interacting with strangers without any sustained anxiety. Following separation from their primary caregiver and then reuniting with their caregiver, *insecurely attached: avoidant* infants can be observed to be excessively clingy, demonstrating extended anxiety and distress. *Insecurely attached: ambivalent* infants may show little consistency in their responses after being separated from and then reunited with their primary caregiver, and may display 'bizarre' and 'contradictory' behaviours such as seeking to be close to their caregiver whilst averting their gaze and 'alternately, engaging with and disengaging from their caregiver almost simultaneously' (Pearce, 2009: 23).

Secure attachment is of course extremely important for children's *happiness* and *wellbeing*, both of which have received much attention in recent decades from academics researching childhood. These two concepts are, however, complex; what, for example, defines happiness and what do we mean by wellbeing? Recently, a major contribution to our understanding of happiness and wellbeing in young children, and how these constructs impact on their learning, has been offered by the *Leuven Wellbeing and Involvement Scales* (Laevers, 2005).

Happiness and wellbeing offer security and a firm basis for later learning

Focus on Theory: Assessing Happiness and Wellbeing

Developed by a team led by Ferre Laevers, the *Leuven Wellbeing and Involvement Scales* have focused on two key indicators of quality provision for children in the Early Years: *wellbeing* and *involvement*. The former is to do with children feeling at ease, being spontaneous and, importantly, feeling free from emotional tensions, all of which are important for effective learning and future mental health. The latter is to do with the levels at which children are seen to be absorbed in activities. In order to measure *wellbeing* and *involvement*, Laevers and his team developed a 5-point scale (for a detailed explanation of this, see www.tes.com/teaching-resource/well-being-and-involvement-leuven-scale-6340990). Practitioners begin their assessment of

> *wellbeing* and *involvement* by observing children individually or in a group for a few minutes and giving a score on the 5-point scale. When children are not scored at Level 4 or 5 their learning is considered to be limited. Where consistently low scores of *wellbeing* and/or *involvement* are recorded then there is a higher probability that aspects of development are under threat; the higher the scores for *wellbeing* and *involvement*, the better social and emotional development and learning will be.
>
> Though the *Leuven Wellbeing and Involvement Scales* offer practitioners a most useful device, they should also be seen as a supplement to critical and objective observation and assessment by those using them.

Case Study Link

The importance of happiness and wellbeing is explored further in Chapters 7, 8, 9 and 10, in Case Studies 7.1, 8.1, 9.1 and 10.1, respectively.

Michael Rutter

Rutter is often referred to as the father of child psychiatry and is recognised for establishing the genetic basis of autism and for heading up the UK Romanian Adoptees Study team, which researched the development of children who had spent their early lives in Romanian orphanages (see Nuffield Foundation, 2009). Rutter found that a significant number of these children who were adopted before six months of age tended to do well in their psychological development as they progressed through adolescence. This finding, amongst his other research into deprivation in childhood, led Rutter to challenge Bowlby's notion that maternal deprivation causes irreversible psychological damage in children (Rutter, 1981). In contrast to Bowlby's views on maternal deprivation, Rutter also asserted that children were able to form multiple attachments as opposed to attaching to one person, typically the child's mother. He further emphasised the fact that maternal deprivation is only one of a range of factors that impact on children's social and emotional development; malnutrition and poverty can also lead to poor emotional and social development in children. Rutter also undertook a study in which he researched the relationship between anti-social behaviour in adolescent boys and maternal separation in early childhood; he observed, for example, that when these boys were given a stable family environment their behaviours improved and anti-social behaviour decreased.

Rudolf Schaffer and Peggy Emerson

An early study by Schaffer and Emerson (1964) concluded that infants were capable of developing multiple attachments; they found that a number of infants in this study became as attached to their fathers as their mothers, with some infants even developing attachment to their father but not their mother despite the fact that it was their mother who was mostly looking after them. They drew many conclusions from their research, suggesting the following stages of attachment:

Stage 1 – *Asocial Stage* (first few weeks). Infants demonstrate similar behaviours towards objects and humans though they can demonstrate some form of preference for familiar adults as indicated by the fact that they are more able to calm them and they present as happier than with other humans.

Stage 2 – *Indiscriminate Attachment* (from 2–7 months). Infants demonstrate increased social behaviours and preference for humans as opposed to objects; they recognise adults and older siblings and demonstrate a preference for familiar others. They are generally accepting of being cuddled and having physical contact with adults, and do not generally demonstrate separation anxiety or anxiety when meeting strangers; because of this, their behaviours relating to attachment can be conceived of as being indiscriminate.

Stage 3 – *Specific Attachment* (from around 7 months). At this stage most infants can be observed to demonstrate anxiety with strangers and when they are separated from their primary familiar adult, most commonly their mother. By this stage they will have developed an attachment to the primary familiar adult, though importantly this adult may not necessarily be the one who is most often with the child, and is rather the one who interacts the most with the child and responds to their different behaviours.

Stage 4 – *Multiple Attachments*. (from 10/11 months plus). Children now begin to demonstrate attachment with one particular adult, though typically they also begin to demonstrate multiple attachments to other adults with whom they spend regular time, which are referred to as 'secondary attachments'. Schaffer and Emerson found that around a third of the children in their study demonstrated secondary attachment after only a month of demonstrating attachment to a primary familiar figure, with most children in their study demonstrating multiple attachments by 12 months.

Activity

View the following two YouTube videos: *How Babies Form Attachments | Four Stages | Schaffer & Emerson*, www.youtube.com/watch?v=WRQiCcH351E (accessed: 16 August 2019); and *Science Bulletins: Attachment Theory— Understanding the Essential Bond*, www.youtube.com/watch?v=kwxjfuPlArY (accessed: 3 August 2020), which offer a detailed explanation of John Bowlby's ideas and how these differed from other theoretical approaches to attachment in childhood. Then, consider what barriers might be created by parents today that impact on strong attachment.

Chapter Summary

- Having positive experiences that promote and extend emotional learning in early childhood is fundamental to building foundations that support later learning and allow for the realisation of potential.
- Much still needs to change so that emotional learning is better understood by those with responsibility for children's learning and education.
- Emotional learning in early childhood underpins most future learning.
- Significant numbers of children in early childhood face barriers that reduce their emotional learning and therefore their formal education.
- Positive attachment is crucial in early childhood and impacts significantly on emotional development and later learning.
- Strong self-efficacy in early childhood is critical to later learning.
- It is important that teachers promote holistic learning in early childhood.

Extended Reading

Bates, B. (2019) *Learning Theories Simplified* (2nd edn). London: Sage. This is a far-reaching and comprehensive text that explores how a very wide range of theoretical approaches attempt to explain aspects of children's learning and development and apply these in practice.

Office for Standards in Education (Ofsted) (2013) *What About the Children? Joint Working between Adult and Children's Services when Parents or Carers have Mental Ill Health and/or Drug and Alcohol Problems*. Manchester: Ofsted. A most informative, relevant, and enlightening account of problems faced by significant numbers of children during childhood.

Page, J. (2014) 'Developing "professional love" in early years settings', in L. Harrison and J. Sumison (eds), *Lived Spaces of Infant-Toddler Education and Care: Exploring Diverse Perspectives on Theory, Research, Practice and Policy*. New York: Springer. A fascinating and informative insight into the importance of professional love within Early Years settings.

3

SOCIAL LEARNING IN CHILDHOOD

By the end of this chapter you should:

- feel confident to describe social development in early childhood
- appreciate how and why social and environmental factors such as poverty and the COVID-19 pandemic impact upon learning in early childhood
- know how to develop strong self-efficacy in young children to support their learning
- understand how language supports effective social learning in early childhood
- be able to articulate how contributions by key theorists have contributed to our understanding of children's social learning and inform thinking and practice

What Does Social Learning Look Like?

Across the globe all children are experiencing social change resulting from the COVID-19 pandemic, which will already be impacting on their social learning in ways that are yet to be understood. We know of course that social learning in childhood is complex and that it varies across communities, societies, and cultures, and will be made even more complex because of this virus. Early Years practitioners and teachers in primary schools, not to mention parents and other professionals such as Health Visitors and Child Psychologists, are now having to grapple with the complex issue of social distancing and how they might support children's social learning whilst keeping them safe and healthy; this is new territory and brings with it enormous challenges for Early Years and primary settings!

Only a few years ago, and prior to the COVID-19 virus emerging, Mercer (2018) illustrated the complex nature of social development when he explained it as:

> A series of changes by which children move from egocentric, self-centred, weakly empathic characteristics of early childhood, when they are unfamiliar with many conventions of social behaviour, to more adult-like characteristics that facilitate empathy, social interactions, relationships with adults and other children, and compliance with conventional standards of behaviour. (p. 166)

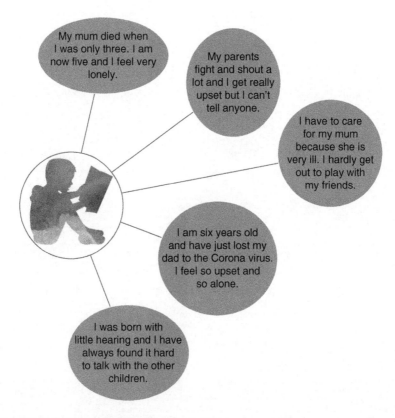

Figure 3.1 Childhood is different for everyone

Some years previously, Fontana (1995) had explained *egocentrism* in childhood as the inability to 'see the world from anything other than a self-centred, subjective viewpoint', and importantly referred to the types of activities that teachers can use to develop empathy, such as role play in drama sessions and encouraging children to develop 'simple imaginative descriptions' (p. 55). Fontana also emphasised that:

> Unless prompted by such activities, some children even at the stage of formal operations seem never to have considered what it must be like to be at the butt of class teasing, or to be old and unwanted, or to grow up against a background of family violence. (p. 247)

In regard to 'compliance with conventional standards of behaviour', this happens naturally, but not all children entering Early Years settings and primary schools will have begun to learn how to comply with standards outside of their homes and may have internalised behaviour patterns modelled to them by dysfunctional parents and older siblings displaying antisocial behaviours. It is now the case that young children are having to comply with and internalise new structures related to COVID-19 that present them with restrictions on what would have previously been considered natural behaviour; keeping social distance from their peers and those adults who manage their learning in different settings is not natural for young children and may, for example, impact on – and even in some cases distort – their natural and emerging dispositions to develop empathy. It is of note that Mercer used the descriptor 'weakly empathic' when referring to very young children; it is also of note that empathy cannot be taught directly and develops at different rates and to different degrees in children depending very much on their upbringing. That said there is much that Early Years practitioners and teachers can do to develop empathy in children, for example by modelling positive responses to different actions, talking through situations sensitively, and explaining clearly the connections between children's actions and consequences. There will be many children, as with Robbie in Case Studies 7.1, 8.1, 9.1 and 10.1 later on, who need adults to support them in developing empathy, and more so given the lessening of social contact created by the COVID-19 pandemic.

Critical Question

What practical steps can Early Years practitioners and teachers in primary schools take to address each of the social changes identified by Mercer in the earlier quotation?

Poverty and its Impact on Social Learning

Poverty affects children's social learning, in ways that all too often go unnoticed and unrecognised. It must be emphasised, however, that not all children born into poverty do badly in terms of their learning (Luke et al., 2020). That said, Cullis and Hansen (2009: 13) noted how very low family incomes can impact on children's learning when they reported that in the UK every £100 of extra income per month, in the first nine months of the lives of children could lead to a difference of a month's development in the children by the time they were five years old. Field (2010) has also reported on the impact of poverty on social learning in childhood and on the life chances of children in the UK when he drew attention to how children:

> ...from low income families in the UK often grow up to be poor adults... [they] are more likely to have pre-school conduct and behavioural problems; more likely to experience bullying and take part in risky behaviours as teenagers; less likely to do well at school; less likely to stay on at school after 16; and more likely to grow up to be poor themselves. (p. 28)

More recently, Sir Michael Wilshaw, the then Chief Inspector (Ofsted) in his annual report (*Unsure Start: HMCI's Early Years Annual Report 2012/13 Speech 2014*) noted how children from the poorest backgrounds '...are less likely to follow instructions, make themselves understood, manage their own basic hygiene or play well together'. He also noted that by the time children start school at five years of age many have started reading simple words and talking in sentences and are able to add single numbers, but that 'far fewer of the poorest can do these things well'. Wilshaw also drew attention to how these children are 'far more likely than their better-off peers to lag behind at age three' and urged a serious note of caution by declaring that 'Too many do badly by the end of primary, and carry on doing badly...' (Wilshaw, 2014: 3).

Case Study Link

Issues raised by Cullis and Hansen, Field, and Wilshaw are explored further in Chapter 9, Case Study 9.1.

Poverty and Diversity

Less than a decade ago, Knowles and Holmström (2013: 162) emphasised the relationship between diversity and poverty by citing the UK government report *A New Approach to Child Poverty: Tackling the Causes of Disadvantage and Transforming Families* (HM Government, 2011: 17), which stated that, at the time, 'Children from black and minority ethnic families are almost twice as likely to live in relative poverty as children from white families'. Knowles and Holmström also drew on evidence from Platt (2007: 1), who had commented on the significant differences between ethnic groups as follows: 'Risks of poverty are highest for Bangladeshis, Pakistanis and Black Africans, but are also above average for Caribbean, Indian and Chinese people. Muslims face higher poverty risks than other religious groups'

(p. 1). Importantly, the HM Government report also drew attention to the relationship between poverty and disability, stating that there were 'around 800,000 children in families with a disabled member in relative poverty'.

Critical Question

How might Early Years practitioners and teachers in primary schools support children whose families are experiencing severe financial hardship resulting from a global downturn in the economy?

Bandura and Social Learning

Bandura (referred to earlier in Chapter 2) is perhaps best known for his *Social Learning* theory (1977) which he later renamed *Social Cognitive Theory* to emphasise the complexity of children's learning. Bandura argued that social factors are central to understanding how children learn. He also believed that motivation is key to learning in childhood and proposed two other important elements in addition to motivation: *imitation* and *identification*. He suggested, for example, that children *imitate* the actions of others and *identify* with individuals they interact with, and in doing so assimilate new learning into existing concepts, which then go some way to structuring how they think and learn. It is through this process that patterns of behaviour become memorised, and this enables children to act in ways they think adults would behave; it is important, therefore, that behaviours modelled to children by adults are positive and appropriate.

Case Study Link

The importance of role modelling is explored further in Chapters 7, 8, 9 and 10, in Case Studies 7.1, 8.1, 9.1 and 10.1, respectively.

Bandura also emphasised how 'symbolic modelling', which is when young children imitate and identify with fictional characters, can be an important source of imitation. Significantly, he emphasised how children not only observe and imitate the physical behaviours of others but also their verbal behaviours and the expectations that adults may have of those around them (Linden, 2005). Children also observe adults as they communicate verbal narratives to others and relate events that have occurred in their own lives or elsewhere, not just verbally but also using gestures.

Having a working lunch! – It's what I see my dad doing

> ### Critical Question
>
> Given the importance Bandura places on imitation, how useful are television and other media for early learning?

Vygotsky and Social Learning

Vygotsky believed that children's learning is essentially experiential. Some years ago, Whitebread (2012) described the central features of Vygotsky's theory most eloquently as follows:

> ...all learning begins in the social context, which supports children in the processes whereby they construct their own understandings... all learning exists first at the 'inter-mental' level in the form of spoken language, and then at the 'intramental' level (i.e. within the child's mind, in the form of internal language, or thought)... This has been termed the 'social constructivist' approach to learning. (p. 127)

The Importance of Culture

Vygotsky placed a great deal of emphasis on culture, which encompasses those social patterns of behaviour and beliefs passed on from one generation to the next through 'cultural tools', by which he meant fairy stories, nursery rhymes, art, and so on. Of course, cultural tools have become more sophisticated in recent decades with the growth of social media, computer and digital technology and television. Vygotsky believed that cultural tools play a significant part in children's thinking and learning, as illustrated some years ago by Pea (1993):

> ...these tools literally carry intelligence in them, in that they represent some individual's or some community's decision that the means thus offered would be reified, made stable as quasi permanent, for the use of others. (p. 52)

Vygotsky also believed that children are born already with the foundations for cognitive development, examples of which are 'visual recognition', 'memory', and 'attention', each of which enables the development of later more complex thinking and learning. Children, he argued, develop their thinking in order that they might apply reason, solve problems they encounter, and apply recall in memory (Rose et al., 2003), all of which are key to later learning.

Critical Question

How might Early Years practitioners and primary teachers be better prepared for recognising barriers to learning in children from BAME backgrounds and what practical steps might they take to develop their knowledge and skills in helping these children overcome barriers?

Learning through Guidance from Others

Vygotsky saw children's development less as an individual process and more as the sum of the relationships children experience with those around them. From birth, he argued, children are immersed in a dynamic, social, and cultural process most typically shaped by the interconnectedness of their relationships with others (Corsaro, 1992). His views on child development have been well encapsulated by Wertsch (1981): 'Children master the social forms of behaviour and transfer these forms to themselves... it is through others that we develop into ourselves...' (p. 164). Vygotsky also believed that infants are born with an innate ability to learn through guidance from others such as their parents and siblings, and, in subsequent years, from Early Years practitioners and teachers who mediate their learning by providing a 'bridge' between their innate ability and more sophisticated learning when they need to interact meaningfully and with accountability within their wider communities. Vygotsky (1978) commented on this process as follows:

> Every function in the child's cultural development appears twice: first, on the social level, and later on the individual level; first, between people (interpsychological), and then inside the child (intrapsychological). (p. 57)

Social activity in childhood, therefore, can be viewed as a bridge across which children move from lower to higher order thinking, involving logical reasoning, intentionality and problem-solving with the support of adults and significant others; lower order thinking largely involves innate biological functions such as memory and attention. It should be emphasised that in regard to this notion of 'bridging', Vygotsky recognised its potential for children who we would now refer to as having additional needs and/or disabilities.

Case Study Link

This notion of teachers acting as a 'bridge' is explored further in Chapter 8, Case Study 8.2.

Bronfenbrenner and Social Learning

Prior to Bronfenbrenner developing his theoretical approach, theorists had typically chosen to focus largely within their respective individual disciplines; child psychologists, for example, focused primarily on the 'child', sociologists on 'the family', anthropologists on 'society', and economists and political scientists on 'economic' and 'political' structures. Bronfenbrenner, in contrast, chose to embrace many disciplines and pull these together in his *Ecological Systems Model*, which he later redefined as the *Bioecological Model*. Bronfenbrenner's ideas differ from other social learning theorists such as Bandura as he placed much greater emphasis on wider political, economic, and cultural factors, arguing that they exert far greater influence on young children and their families. Unlike Bandura's theory of *Social Learning*, Bronfenbrenner emphasised the important role that children's own biologies play in their learning and the interrelationship between these and the communities, societies and cultures in which children grow up (Bronfenbrenner, 1979; Bronfenbrenner and Ceci, 1994). It is useful at this point to look at Bronfenbrenner's concept of layers (Figure 3.2), which models his theoretical approach, and which is often likened to a 'Russian doll'.

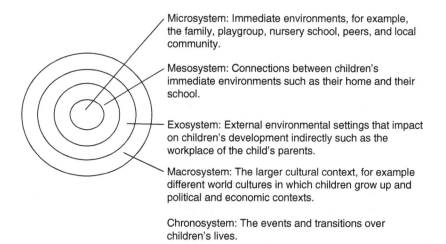

Figure 3.2 Bronfenbrenner's Ecological Systems Model of Individual Development

> ## Focus on Theory: Bronfenbrenner's Ecological Systems Model
>
> The inner layer is the **Microsystem**, which can be recognised as a child's immediate environments, for example family, pre-school, peer group and immediate neighbourhood. Bronfenbrenner proposed a two-way process within this layer, which he referred to as 'bi-directional influences' where children are influenced by the behaviours of their parents but also in turn influence their parents' behaviours. Next is the **Mesosystem**: comprising connections between a child's immediate environments, for example their home and their pre-school or junior school. Here, a child learns to relate experiences gained in their nursery or primary school to those of their family and in doing so may form comparisons between teachers and their parents and between new nursery or school friends and those back in their immediate communities and between their siblings. The **Exosystem** refers to those external environmental settings which impact indirectly on development, for example the nature of their parents' employment, the physical environment where they live, their friends and neighbours and even extended family members living quite some distance away. The **Macrosystem** refers to wider contexts, for example, the economy, political change and historical cultures and subcultures. The **Chronosystem** can be viewed as those environmental events over time that impact on the child and the transitions they experience in their lives. The lives of young children change significantly when they start playgroup and then primary school. Some children may in their Early Years transition from a two-parent to a single-parent household following their parents' separation or divorce.

Discussion Point

How might Bronfenbrenner's *Ecological Model* help to explain the impact of the COVID-19 pandemic on children's learning?

Rogoff and Social Learning

Like Vygotsky, Barbara Rogoff (2003) has emphasised how children develop as participants in their cultural communities; she sees development as not just happening within children themselves but within dynamic group and community processes of which children are an integral part. She argues that to properly understand developmental growth and learning in early childhood we need to study it not only within family life but also within community and cultural practices. In emphasising the importance of examining perspectives of children from different cultures and communities, Rogoff underscores the value of learning from both 'insiders' and 'outsiders' who make up communities.

We can see that Rogoff's approach to understanding developmental growth and learning in childhood also requires that we explore the perspectives of a range of individuals who make up families and communities, including the children themselves. She emphasises that it is important also to acknowledge that children are capable of holding opinions and ideas, and that their perspectives as 'insiders' in families and their wider communities are essential when attempting to understand and explain the complex issues that impact on children as they grow up.

Emphasising the importance of social context and environment on learning, she has stressed the value of seeing how children learn alongside others, both adults and children. She draws attention to how children develop as participants in their cultural communities, and therefore how development occurs not only within children themselves but within and through group and community processes. If we want to understand learning and development, she argues, then we need to explore these elements within family life and community practices. Rogoff has also emphasised the importance of taking the different perspectives of children's development into account that are found across cultures and communities.

Play offers wonderful opportunities for social learning

Gopnik and Social Learning

In recent years the work of Alison Gopnik (Gopnik, 2009; Gopnik, 2012; Gopnik et al., 2001) has influenced how many think about learning in young children; she has also challenged many of the traditional ways that have sought to explain learning in early childhood. Recently, Gray and MacBlain (2015) drew attention to this aspect of Gopnik's work as follows:

Gopnik (2009, p. 6) notes that, until recently, philosophers rarely mentioned babies, infants, families, parents, mothers or fathers... She argues for a new look at babies, and a new view of babies based on philosophical ideas. (p. 20)

Gray and MacBlain go on to indicate how Gopnik has claimed that '...children develop their own theories of how the world is constructed, test their ideas and draw conclusions based on the evidence', and because of this '...she describes them as philosophers, researchers and theorists' (p. 21). Gray and MacBlain (2015: 21) have also noted how Gopnik (2009: 8) has drawn upon her own experiences, observations and experiments to conclude that 'Learning is about the way the world changes our mind, but our minds can also change the world'.

Gopnik emphasises the need to accept that children think differently and has argued that adults are programmed to find solutions as opposed to creating solutions when faced with tasks that require them to problem-solve. In this way, their thinking is qualitatively different to that of young children, who approach problem-solving tasks more creatively; this suggests that we give more credence to the nature of children's thinking as, unlike adults, they do not typically focus on finding solutions. She also argues that infants and very young children express their intelligence through explorations with their environments and with those around them, and less through formal settings such as classrooms where they are expected to respond to adult-led teaching.

Activity

View the following link: *How Babies Think*, Alison Gopnik, available at: http://alisongopnik.com/Papers_Alison/sciam-Gopnik.pdf (accessed: 2 March 2020). Then, consider how her views differ from those of the early *behaviourists* who saw all behaviour as being learned.

Language and Social Learning

It is through language, both verbal and non-verbal, that we communicate with those around us and develop as social beings. We know that new-born infants are already programmed to acquire language, which they then develop, and that language is central to learning in early childhood, but worryingly the picture in the UK has reflected major issues in regard to children's language development. Some years ago, Palmer (2006), for example, felt able to write:

> Everywhere I went it was the same story: four- and five-year-olds were coming to school with poorer language skills than ever before; they weren't arriving with the

repertoire of nursery rhymes and songs little ones always used to know, and children of all ages found it increasingly difficult to sit down and listen to their teacher or to express complex ideas in speech or writing… (p. 105)

More recently, Save the Children in 2018 made reference to how 'One child in five starts primary school in England without the language skills they need to succeed, a figure that rises to one in three of the poorest children (Department for Education 2015)'. Their study was based on findings from an analysis of the Millennium Cohort Study (IOE, 2014) undertaken by the UCL Institute of Education for Save the Children, which explored the relationship between the language skills of five year olds beginning primary school and their subsequent attainments in English and mathematics at ages seven and eleven. Their findings revealed that one in four children who struggled with language at five years of age failed to reach the expected standard in English by the time they left primary school, compared with one in twenty-five children who had demonstrated good language skills at five, and one in five the expected standard in mathematics as compared with one in fifty who had demonstrated good language skills at five. To gain a better understanding of language development in children it is important to look at contrasting approaches; we begin with those of the *behaviourist* tradition and of Noam Chomsky, followed by an exploration of Vygotsky's thoughts on language.

Chomsky and the Behaviourist Tradition

As we have already seen, the ideas of the *behaviourists* came to dominate thinking and practice in the years following World War II, at the heart of which lay the idea that all behaviour is learned, including language, which is learned through 'imitation'. Jones (2016) has articulated the *behaviourist* position regarding language as follows:

> The theory put forward by the *behaviourists* suggests that, for example, babies hear a variety of common speech sounds around them and when they accidentally use some of these sounds, parents respond with delight and praise, which rewards the child and spurs him on to repeat the behaviour… (p. 14)

Chomsky (1965) challenged the ideas of the *behaviourists* arguing that children do not simply learn language by imitating those around them but instead, they create language themselves. He proposed that children's acquisition of language follows patterns, for example acquiring grammatical rules, and that this process is derived from what he termed the 'Language Acquisition Device' that is innate and genetically determined. Jones (2016) has illustrated Chomsky's position most eloquently, as follows:

> Chomsky and adherents to his theory emphasise that language acquisition is an innate feature of human development, i.e. genetically determined. They also argue that much of children's language is acquired despite the seemingly chaotic nature of what they hear being said to them and around them. (p. 18)

However, Chomsky and adherents to his theory also recognise, as Jones indicates, that there 'must also be an element of imitation' (p. 19). Of course, we know that when young children play, they are also introduced to new models and patterns of language that we can observe them imitating. In this way, we can see the importance of play and how language is a fundamental aspect not only of development, but also, importantly, of learning.

Children learn to communicate with their worlds in all manner of ways

Vygotsky and Social Language

Vygotsky proposed that it is through talking and listening to others that children develop as social beings and come to understand the world they are growing up in. Indeed, the importance he attached to how language enables this process to unfold can be seen in his own words:

> The structure of speech is not simply the mirror image of the structure of thought. It cannot, therefore, be placed on thought like clothes off a rack. Speech does not merely serve as the expression of developed thought. Thought is restructured as it is transformed into speech. It is not expressed but completed in the word. (Vygotsky, 1987, quoted in Holzman, 2006: 115)

Vygotsky saw language as the means of transmitting meaning, as it is through language that children engage with others by interpreting what they hear and say; through this process, they contribute to their communities and to the wider societies in which they live. It is this reciprocal process of constructing meaning through social action that lies at the very heart of Vygotsky's theory of *Social Constructivism*, which Whitebread (2012) articulated earlier in this chapter, as follows:

> ...all learning begins in the social context, which supports children in the processes whereby they construct their own understandings... all learning exists first at the 'inter-mental' level in the form of spoken language, and then at the 'intramental' level (i.e. within the child's mind, in the form of internal language, or thought)... This has been termed the 'social constructivist' approach to learning. (p. 127)

Central to Vygotsky's explanations of children's learning are four stages in the development of language, which unlike Piaget's notion of stages are not unidirectional, but rather develop progressively, following an incremental pathway. As children's cognitive development matures and as they gain from their experiences of the world around them, they can move backwards as well as forwards between stages. Gray and MacBlain (2015) have described Vygotsky's stages as follows:

> **Primitive stage:** Children under 2 years of age use vocal activity as a means of emotional expression and for social engagement... behaviour becomes increasingly purposeful and goal-directed... thought and language are separate...
>
> **Practical intelligence:** ...the child's language uses syntactic (rules of speech) and logical forms. These forms of speech are linked to the child's practical problem-solving activities...
>
> **External symbolic stage:** Thinking aloud is common... [it] enables the child to self-regulate and plan their activities...
>
> **Internalization of symbolic tools:** Between 7 and 8 years of age... Problem solving continues to be guided by speech... leads to greater cognitive independence, flexibility, and freedom... (p. 97)

Activity

How might Early Years practitioners and primary teachers support children at each of Vygotsky's stages who are presenting with speech and language difficulties, and what other professionals might they need to involve, if any?

Whilst we can explore what is considered to be the normal course of language development it is also important to recognise that there are those children whose problems with language are not to do simply with delay and poor experiences in early childhood, but do in fact derive from more specific underlying difficulties, for example those with dyspraxia and dyslexia, and those children on the autistic spectrum (these issues are explored in Chapter 9, Case Study 9.2, and Chapter 10, Case Study 10.1). For these children it will be essential that Early Years practitioners and teachers inform themselves about the types of difficulties these children will experience in order that appropriate assessment of their needs can be arranged and effective interventions put in place; in some instances, referrals to external agencies such as Speech and Language Therapy and Educational Psychology services may be necessary.

Case Study Link

The complexity of language development in early childhood is explored more fully in Chapters 9 and 10, in Case Studies 9.1, 9.2 and 10.1.

The Ethics of Care

Nel Noddings

Central to social learning in early childhood is the importance of 'care' and children needing to feel they are cared for. Being cared for impacts significantly on how children relate to others not only in childhood but also in later life. In recent decades, the celebrated American philosopher Nel Noddings (infed.org, 2018) has drawn attention to the importance of children receiving appropriate care in their first months and years, and how this impacts on their social learning. Noddings sees the primary purpose of education to be that of creating caring, confident, and loving individuals. Interestingly, she has drawn a distinction between the nature of caring in early education, which she refers to as caring in a 'virtue' sense and caring in the 'relational' sense. With the first of these, teachers will be conscientious, following goals and objectives for their pupils whilst working hard to inspire them to achieve goals and succeed academically, though some teachers may not be able to establish relations of 'care and trust' in what Noddings calls the 'relational sense' where teachers employ high levels of empathy and see each child as a unique individual. Importantly, she has suggested that some teachers may find it difficult to demonstrate relational caring due to the strong legacy in teaching where many teachers feel they know best, a view that she emphasises is unacceptable today.

Noddings has also emphasised the challenges facing teachers today who have to manage the complex nature of some children's conditions; this, in addition to managing external factors such as large class sizes, imposed curricula, an increased emphasis on and frequency of testing and achieving targets, and standardised testing (Aubrey and Riley,

2017). Hope (2018) has picked up on these last points and drawn attention to how teachers in the UK struggle to achieve a balance between delivering curricula that are largely target-driven whilst also meeting the social and emotional needs of their pupils:

> The need to maximize every moment of potential learning time can lead to classrooms that minimize the human needs of teachers and learners and pressurize both leading to anxiety, stress and potential unhappiness. (p. 25)

This is a point also emphasised by Roffey et al. (2016), who have drawn attention to the potential conflicts between nurturing children's emotional development and meeting externally imposed targets, as follows: 'Teachers these days are judged on academic outcomes but rarely on the difference they make to someone's life' (p. 240).

Discussion Point

Do all teachers care?

Behaviourism and its Relevance for Social Learning Today

Behaviour Modification and Operant Conditioning

Whilst *behaviourism* came to dominate much practice in the past it arguably went out of favour in recent decades; it does, however, have a great deal to offer Early Years practitioners and teachers today in understanding and explaining social learning in childhood. Every day, Early Years practitioners and teachers modify children's behaviour, often without realising they are doing so. They do this primarily through reinforcing the behaviours of children by, for example, offering positive consequences to their behaviours through smiling and giving verbal praise; they also reward specific behaviours with such techniques as 'star charts' and 'smiley-faces'. It is through modifying intentional behaviours that adults subtly shape children's behaviours, and therefore their social learning.

Behaviour modification has its origins in *behaviourism*, and most notably perhaps the work of Skinner (1953; 1957), who recognised how reinforcement that is positive strengthens children's behaviours while reinforcement that is negative lessens behaviours. Skinner noted how the frequency with which reinforcement followed behavioural responses was a key factor in increasing desired behaviours. Learning occurs where behaviours initiated are rewarded or punished and where associations are formed between behaviours and their consequences. Adults who have a good understanding of *operant conditioning* can knowingly modify children's behaviour, referred to as *behaviour modification*.

Chapter Summary

- Every child's social experiences are different and impact differently on intellectual and emotional development.
- Social development in early childhood is shaped by internal as well as external factors.
- Social development impacts on cognitive development and learning in early childhood.
- Students and trainees studying to become Early Years practitioners and teachers need to understand how environmental factors can shape social learning in early childhood.
- Young children need to be supported with developing strong self-efficacy, which will impact on their future learning.
- The behaviourist approach has a great deal to offer Early Years practitioners and teachers in their attempts at developing children's social learning.

Extended Reading

Allott, K. and Waugh, D. (2019) 'Talk and communication: couldn't they just sit down and shut up', in C. Carden (ed.), *Primary Teaching*. London: Sage. A concise chapter that explores the nature of talk in the classroom and its link to behaviour.

Jones, M. (2016) *Talking and Learning with Young Children*. London: Sage. This is an excellent book; extremely interesting and readable. It gives a comprehensive and most accessible account of the relationship between learning and talking in early childhood.

Knowles, G. and Holmström, R. (2013) *Understanding Family Diversity and Home-School Relations: A Guide for Students and Practitioners in Early Years and Primary Settings*. London: Routledge. An accessible text that explores how practitioners and teachers can develop effective partnerships with families and support children's learning by embracing the diversity of family life.

4

COGNITIVE DEVELOPMENT AND LEARNING

By the end of this chapter you should:

- understand how legacies left to us by philosophers and theorists continue to influence practice
- appreciate how the current COVID-19 pandemic is impacting on cognitive development and learning in early childhood
- know that cognitive development and learning are complex and require Early Years practitioners and teachers to have a sound theoretical knowledge
- understand why play in childhood needs to be better understood as a pedagogic approach
- fully appreciate the potential that outdoor play has for learning in early childhood

Intellectual Development

Piaget (1896–1980)

In many respects, Jean Piaget revolutionised thinking and practice in the Early Years and drew attention to the importance of recognising how children act on their environments and, in doing so, construct learning. Rose and Wood (2016) recently illustrated this point when they noted that 'Piaget argued that children are intrinsically motivated to learn and actively construct their own meaning, hence the term 'constructivism' (p. 95). Piaget believed that by interacting with their environments, children create internal mental representations, which he referred to as *schema*, which Nutbrown (2006: 7) has explained as 'a way of labelling children's consistent patterns of action'. By observing *schema*, Early Years practitioners and teachers in primary schools can familiarise themselves with how individual children approach learning, the type of things that motivate them and what opportunities and environments best support their learning. It is important, however, to differentiate *schema* from *concepts*; Hayes (1994: 143–4) has helped us to make this distinction when she described *schema* as being like cognitive maps that enable children to engage in activities such as planning, whilst *concepts* enable children to classify phenomena, for example objects they see and play with and events that take place around them. Fontana (1995) has underlined the importance of concepts in children's thinking by explaining that they help children make sense of their worlds:

> ...a small child will have a concept of 'big things'... a concept of 'wetness'... a concept of 'things I like' and of 'things I don't like', and so on. When encountering novel objects or experiences, or faced with problems of any kind, a child attempts to make sense of them by fitting them into the range of concepts already held. If these concepts prove inadequate, he or she may have to modify them in some way, or perhaps try to develop a new concept altogether. (p. 51)

Piaget placed great emphasis on how children 'act on' their environments (Hayes, 1994: 143–4), which he argued is central to how children think. By acting on their environments, children, he believed, 'assimilate' and then 'accommodate' new information, which guides their behaviours and, therefore, their learning.

Focus on Theory: Piaget and Cognitive Development in Childhood

Piaget believed that cognitive development follows a set of stages that are 'invariant'; i.e. children pass through one stage before progressing to the next. The first of these is the *sensorimotor Stage* (0–2 years) when children learn through their senses, followed by the *preoperational Stage* (2–7 years) when language allows for the rapid growth of schema through *assimilation* and *accommodation*. It is through acting on their environments that children assimilate and then accommodate information that is new to them, and it is this process that guides their learning. *Assimilation* can be understood as new information that is absorbed by children into their schemas without any real manipulation of that information taking place. In contrast, *accommodation* is where relevant schemas then adapt in order that this new information can be stored. This second stage comprises two further sub-stages, the *preconceptual* (2–4 years) and the *intuitive* (4–7 years). In the former, children increasingly engage in imaginative and symbolic play, which involves the increasing use of words and symbols to represent objects or people (Gray and MacBlain, 2015; MacBlain, 2018). Piaget suggested that it is during the later *intuitive stage* that children develop their cognitive skills and abilities to levels that allow them to remove themselves from learning situations and view the whole, as opposed to focusing on detail; he referred to this as *decentring*. He acknowledged, however, that children's thinking remains limited at this stage; a child at this stage who observes an adult pouring a fixed amount of water from a short fat glass into a long slim glass will typically believe there is more water in the long slim glass. Piaget referred to this type of thinking as *conservation*, and believed that a child's ability to conserve denotes the end of the *preoperational stage* and the beginning of the *concrete operational stage* (7–11 years) when thinking becomes more flexible and children are learning to apply logic when engaged in problem-solving activities, though their thinking remains limited by a need to have concrete objects at hand. The *concrete operational stage* is then followed by the *formal operational stage* (11–15 years) when thinking is much more flexible and symbolic and is not limited to physical experiences; through their thinking and use of language children at this stage can now apply logic when engaging in deductive reasoning as they test out hypotheses and engage in reflection.

It is through imaginative play that we learn to make sense of the world around us

Vygotsky (1896–1934)

Lev Vygotsky has offered a great deal to our understanding of learning in early childhood and though his ideas differ in many ways from those of Piaget there are also many similarities. Vygotsky believed that cognition in children develops through their interactions with others. He also believed that children are born already with the foundations for thinking and with the capacity to learn through guidance from others; this capacity to learn from others, he maintained, facilitates the passing on of cultural norms that are intrinsic to the communities and cultures into which children are born and the societies in which they grow up and which shape their intellectual development and, therefore, their learning. Vygotsky proposed that every function in the cultural development of children '…appears twice: first, on the social level, and later, the individual level; first, between people… and then inside the child…' (Vygotsky, 1978: 57). This statement reflects the extremely high level of significance he placed on social learning as being prerequisite to later individualised learning.

Bruner (1915–2016)

Like Piaget and Vygotsky, Jerome Bruner (1960, 1983) has offered much to how we understand learning in childhood. At the centre of Bruner's theoretical approach is the notion of *instrumental conceptualism*, which is characterised by three key fundamentals: *acquiring new information or knowledge*; *transforming and manipulating knowledge*; and *the checking of knowledge*. His ideas on learning have been articulated most concisely by Brown (1977), as follows:

> Bruner's thesis was that the study of children in problem-solving situations had concentrated too much on the nature of the tasks and the stimuli presented to the child, and too little on the dynamic qualities the child brought to the tasks in order to solve them. (p. 74)

Bruner proposed that children represent their worlds through three modes, *enactive*, which refers to actions by young children, *iconic*, which refers to images and pictures, and *symbolic*, which refers to words and symbols. These modes do not follow on from one another as in Piaget's stages of cognitive development, but rather are integral to one another and linked to the nature of children's life experiences.

The Enactive Mode

Here, a new-born child's view of objects becomes connected to their physical movements. Take a situation where an infant lying in a cot is given a rattle; when she shakes the rattle, it makes a sound, and she is then alerted to the sound. Over time, her physical movements become linked to the sight and sound of the rattle itself and will be gradually encoded into the infant's memory store in what is commonly referred to as 'kinaesthetic memory'.

The Iconic Mode

In this mode, children represent objects as images, which allows them to advance their thinking. They can then think of objects and people not immediately present in their environment. This mode is, however, limited because images that are internally represented and stored are restricted to observable features such as colour and size and shape and smell. A further limitation of the *iconic* mode is that it does not allow for the representation and storing of abstract concepts, such as sadness and happiness.

The Symbolic Mode

For abstract concepts to be stored, children need language, and it is this fundamental point that is central to understanding the *symbolic* mode. Brown (1977) offered the following extremely useful example, which explains the difference between images in the *iconic* mode and symbols in the *symbolic* mode, as follows:

> A photograph or a model of a cow would be an icon in that it would represent the animal in a very real and obvious way. The symbols C-O-W have no such characteristics. They only signify the existence of the animal by consensus of those who use the word. (p. 75)

With the development of language children are increasingly able to remove themselves physically from situations whilst still thinking about aspects of the situation. They are also able to communicate with others about events that are not physically present in their environment and that are happening elsewhere or in the future. Importantly, they can purposefully join in problem-solving activities, and in reflection.

Scaffolding

Like Vygotsky, Bruner was interested in how children can be supported when approaching new learning tasks and when engaged in problem-solving activities, and how their learning can be improved through guidance from adults. Though originally coined by Wood et al. (1976), cited in Gray and MacBlain (2015: 6), the term *scaffolding* is largely associated with Bruner and refers to a process whereby adults working alongside children support and progress their learning. *Scaffolding* can be extremely effective as well as highly motivating for children, and amongst its many benefits is the fact that it is flexible and can be used by adults in most situations. It can be particularly beneficial where adults work alongside children with special educational needs and/or disabilities.

Gardner

Howard Gardner (1983) has offered an appealing and alternative view to what has been traditionally understood as intelligence. For Gardner, intelligence needs to be seen not as a single or unitary concept but instead as 'multiple intelligences' with each of these being 'a system in its own right' but which need to interact with each other, as without interaction 'nothing could be achieved' (p. 851). Gardner summarised his multiple intelligences as 'Linguistic', 'Logical-Mathematical', 'Spatial, Musical', 'Bodily-Kinaesthetic', 'Interpersonal' and 'Intrapersonal'; more recently, he has suggested that there may be others such as 'Naturalist intelligence'.

It should be noted that whilst Gardner's ideas have been embraced by many Early Years practitioners and teachers (Smith, 2002/2008) his ideas have also been open to criticism (Schaler, 2006). His notion of 'multiple intelligences' has, for example, been criticised by those who argue that it lacks 'testability', which results from 'an ambiguity of the theory, in that it is not clear to what extent the intelligences are supposed to operate separately or interconnectedly' (Brooks et al., 2004: 55). Aubrey and Riley (2017) have also drawn attention to 'the lack of empirical evidence available to support his claims, with the suggestion that Gardner's work is founded on his own intuition and reasoning rather than any research evidence' (p. 157). They go on to emphasise, however, that Gardner has been willing to amend his theory in response to criticism from others. Aubrey and Riley have also sought to contextualise Gardner's ideas within recent political changes in the UK by drawing attention to how, since 2010, there has been a return by successive governments 'to a more formal curriculum, in which subjects were to be taught as disciplines… and in which there was a heavy emphasis on the core subjects of English and mathematics and science' (p. 157), which has worked against practitioners and teachers applying Gardner's ideas as 'the creative curriculum was never fully realised' (p. 157).

Freire (1921–1997)

Paulo Freire was a Brazilian educationalist who viewed education not just as a means of achieving academic qualifications and skills but importantly as a means of helping children understand their social worlds and, more particularly, social problems and how they themselves might in the future become agents of social change. Freire proposed that teachers who see themselves as holding greater power than their pupils because of their qualifications and who do not recognise their own infallibility put themselves unwittingly in positions where their thinking becomes limited and rigid. In essence, they display themselves as being the sole person in the learning dynamic who possesses the knowledge, whilst their pupils do not; this, Freier argues, militates against children's education being a process that truly facilitates and encourages active enquiry.

The Banking Method

Freire was critical of teachers who believe they hold all the answers and who perceive their pupils to be empty vessels which need to be filled with knowledge; he referred to this pedagogical approach as the *banking method*, where children are seen more as objects than as complex individuals with dynamic identities who have their own valid ways of learning and thinking. With the *banking method*, children, he argued, are not encouraged to think critically or to develop confidence in how they themselves think. Such an approach, he asserted, leads teachers to believe that they need to maintain a hierarchical structure in learning situations where they continue to exercise control over their pupils.

Critical Pedagogy: Learning through Problems

In contrast to the *banking method*, Freire promoted *critical pedagogy* where teachers and children are, seen as equals and where dialogue is central to learning. At the centre of this type of pedagogical approach lies the importance of problematising issues that pupils are introduced to by their teachers; in this way, children come to understand that simplistic and universally agreed answers do not exist, and that answers to the bigger questions in life are complex and require much critical reflection and engagement with ideas that are promoted by others, and that teachers do not have all the answers.

The Importance of Dialogue

Two key features in Freire's pedagogical approach are the importance of dialogue and children learning about themselves through having respect for others. Importantly, he also emphasised that for children, dialogue should not be artificially imposed. Through positive dialogue children learn to tolerate the thinking and actions of others and, in turn, learn from others. He believed that imposing our own views on others is indicative of low self-confidence in what we ourselves believe; when used with purpose, dialogue can underpin sound pedagogical practice characterised by critical thinking and improved abilities in problem-solving. Through dialogue children understand that different answers to questions are possible and that there are alternatives to what others assert is the truth; importantly, children learn to listen to and reflect on alternative views, and in this way develop their own critical thinking.

Through play, children can model the worlds they live in

Play as a Pedagogic Approach

The concept of play and the degree to which it is or is not inseparable from cognitive development and learning in childhood has been debated by philosophers, theorists, and practitioners for generations (Nutbrown and Clough, 2014) and continues to be so. The distinction between those who advocate for play as central to learning in the Early Years and those who wish for a more formalised approach to early learning was exemplified some years ago when in February 2012 Graeme Paton, education editor for the national online UK newspaper *The Telegraph*, brought to the public's attention the following:

> In a letter to *The Daily Telegraph*, academics and authors said that controversial education reforms are robbing under-fives of the ability to play and leading to the 'schoolification' of the early years... The experts... suggested the system was 'too inflexible to cater for the highly diverse developmental needs of young children'.

More recently, this distinction has again been highlighted by the National Association of Head Teachers (NAHT) when delegates at their annual conference in 2018 voted overwhelmingly in support of a motion that was highly critical of the recent Ofsted publication, *Bold Beginnings*, which focused on learning in early childhood. The NAHT offered the following on their website (2018):

> *Ofsted's recent Bold Beginnings report on teaching in the reception year has provided some deeply flawed analysis based on limited evidence. Conference is asked to reject an interpretation of early years education that:*
>
> - *fails to acknowledge the wealth of evidence and research that the role of play is crucial in children's learning as part of the curriculum;*
> - *requires four-year-old children to sit and undertake formal work too early...*

Wood (2008) cited in Nutbrown and Clough (2014: 154) has also highlighted the distinction in children's play and learning, indicating that:

> While there is substantial evidence on learning through play, there has been less evidence on teaching through play. Linking play and pedagogy has long been a contentious area, because of the ideological commitment to free play and free choice. (Nutbrown and Clough: 27)

Wood goes on to propose how:

> ...contemporary theoretical and policy changes have shifted the focus to better understanding the distinctive purposes and nature of play in education settings, and the role of adults in planning for play and playfulness in child-initiated or teacher-directed activities. (Nutbrown and Clough: 154)

A further helpful approach to explaining children's play and learning has been offered by Smith et al. (2003) who made a key distinction between play and exploration in very young children, which can in part be located within the ideas of the *behaviourists* and their emphasis on 'reinforcement', and those who have promoted the more stage-based theoretical approach offered by Piaget:

> Both exploration and play were awkward for traditional learning theorists, as neither was obviously goal seeking or under the control of reinforcers. It is also true that with very young children, during sensori motor development… the distinction between exploration and play is difficult to make, as for young infants, all objects are novel. By the preschool years, however, the distinction is clearer. (p. 218)

Critical Question

What types of behaviours might Early Years practitioners and teachers in primary schools look for in children's play that suggest new learning is taking place, and how might they record these?

Pramling Samuelsson

Ingrid Pramling Samuelsson is a Swedish academic who has written extensively about children's learning and early development. Though based on the Scandinavian system her work offers a useful frame of reference against which practice in the UK can be compared. With her co-author Asplund Carlsson (Pramling Samuelsson and Asplund Carlsson, 2008: 1) she drew attention to the debate around play and learning in early childhood by emphasising '…how play and learning are related is almost never discussed…'. They also drew attention to how teachers '…often get too "teacherly" in their efforts…' when working with young children. They have also highlighted important distinctions that children make in their play, a point also emphasised by Smith et al. (2003) who, for example, distinguished 'language play' from other types of play, and that emphasises those differences in types of play suggested by Smith et al. (2003), who distinguished 'language play' from other types of play and early exploration: '…when young children *act* they do not separate between play and learning, although they separate them in their talk…'. Importantly, they have also reported on how some young children:

> who have been involved in a pedagogy where play and learning become integrated do not even make a distinction between play and learning when they are asked about it in primary school. (p. 2)

> **Activity**
>
> View Pramling Samuelsson and Asplund Carlsson's article, 'The playing learning child: towards a pedagogy of early childhood', available at: www.researchgate.net/publication/215473204_The_Playing_Learning_Child_Towards_a_pedagogy_of_early_childhood (accessed: 3 October 2020), which offers some excellent case studies of learning and play in early childhood, and then view the Ofsted publication, *Bold Beginnings*, available at: https://assets.publishing.service.gov.uk/government/uploads/system/uploads/attachment_data/file/663560/28933_Ofsted_-_Early_Years_Curriculum_Report_-_Accessible.pdf (accessed: 3 October 2020). Having looked at both sources, reflect on why you think their views might be different.

Nutbrown

Cathy Nutbrown has been a hugely influential figure in the field of early learning, and her contribution to our understanding of learning and play in childhood has inspired many practitioners over the years. Amongst her many and substantial contributions has been her emphasis on the importance of quality opportunities for young children in their learning and the need for adults working with young children to be informed and well-trained. Like others, Nutbrown has recognised the debate that continues to exist in the UK over the role of play in children's learning. She has focused attention on how professionals working in the Early Years sector are trained and the importance of training courses giving greater credence to play and how adults can best support children's learning through play. Contextualising her views, she has also emphasised how adults observing children at play do not always comprehend what they are seeing, with children willing only sometimes '…to explain what they are doing'. Nutbrown also emphasised how adults working with young children should have greater expertise '…in knowing when to step in and join children as they play and when to step aside and allow children to follow their own pursuits unhindered'.

> **Activity**
>
> Take time to view the following link, *How to Identify Schemas in Play: Cathy Nutbrown Interview – A Powerful Tool for Any Early Years Practitioner*, available at: https://famly.co/blog/management/identify-schemas-in-play-cathy-nutbrown/ (accessed: 3 October 2020). Then, take time to consider why some adults might struggle to see the full value of play in children's learning.

Viewing Learning from the Child's Perspective

Moyles

Janet Moyles (1989) has been a strong voice in understanding the benefits that free play and directed play have for learning in early childhood. At the centre of her ideas is the notion of the 'play spiral'. She suggests, for example, that directed play can be used to teach children knowledge and skills and, importantly, that learning acquired through this process can be built on and reinforced through free play.

Case Study Link

The value of free play for children's learning is explored in Chapter 6, Case Study 6.1.

Moyles promoted the idea that through repetition of directed play and free play there emerges a 'spiral' in children's learning, thus:

> Rather like a pebble on a pond, the ripples from the exploratory free play through directed play and back to enhanced and enriched free play, allowed a spiral of learning ever outwards into wider experiences for the children and upwards into the accretion of knowledge and skills. (Moyles, 1989: 15)

This concept of a 'spiral' is helpful as it creates an image of actions engaged in by children leading to wider learning. It also reinforces the importance of children being able to interact with their environments and learning through this process of interaction when not being overly directed; here, we can identify similarities between many of the theoretical approaches offered by a range of theorists.

Activity

Take time to view the following report, *Unhurried Pathways: A New Framework for Early Childhood*, Early Childhood Action Winchester, October 2012, available at: https://deyproject.files.wordpress.com/2012/06/eca-eyf-unhurried-pathways.pdf (accessed: 3 October 2020), in which Moyles has written the Foreword, then consider the key points in this document against your own views of current practice in the UK. Give some thought to why a 'new' framework was felt necessary and what factors would have led policy makers to believe that a new framework was called for.

Play out of doors offers wonderful opportunities for integration of the senses

Learning: Can We Really Make It Happen Out Of Doors?

There has been a considerable growth in our understanding of the benefits that outdoor provision and learning can offer children in their Early Years. I (the author) was fortunate enough to be lecturing at Bridgwater College in Somerset in the 1990s where my colleagues introduced the idea of 'Forest Schools' to the UK for the first time. It was a real joy to see their enthusiasm as they introduced the concept within the college's Children's Centre after their initial visits to Scandinavia. In my practice as an Educational Psychologist I have also seen at first hand the value of outdoor experiences for young children and how these experiences impacted significantly and positively on children's learning.

> ### Critical Question
>
> What practical steps might Early Years practitioners and teachers in primary schools take to support the learning of children with sensory impairment out of doors?

Bilton

Helen Bilton with co-author Jane Waters (Bilton and Waters, 2016) have explained *outdoor provision* and *outdoor learning* as those experiences 'that children have when outside during curriculum time, that is experiences that have been planned and are framed by the adults' intentions for children's learning' (p. 3). However, they also emphasise that their explanation does not refer to those times when children have breaks outside such as their playtimes during the mornings and afternoons; rather, they refer to outdoor learning as learning activities that are planned and that '...may be organised within the confines of the school environment and beyond, including playful encounters with materials, objects and equipment' (p. 3). Importantly, Bilton and Waters (2016) have drawn attention to how the *English Early Years Statutory Framework* enshrined the outdoor environment in statute, with the *Foundation Phase Framework for Children's Learning* for 3–7 year olds in Wales making an explicit requirement for children in this age range to have significant access to outdoor provision. However, they also emphasise how 'most recently the emphasis on this space has been significantly lessened under English legislation' (p. 3).

Bilton and Waters make reference to a survey undertaken by Bilton in 2014, which looked at the 'professed aims of Early Years teachers in South East England' and indicated how many teachers were unclear as to the aims of outdoor education, and that some confused aims with actions taking place within their settings. They also drew attention to how Maynard and Waters (2007) had highlighted an ambiguity amongst teachers regarding their understanding of the purpose of outdoor provision. With regard to the situation in England, Bilton and Waters have suggested that '...it would seem wasteful to present evidence that outdoor learning is very important and only a few years later to ignore this evidence' (p. 3). They go on to assert that:

> ...for both England and Wales it would seem of benefit to make clearer... the necessary link between the aim or purpose of education and the planned learning outcomes for children, given there is now strong evidence that high quality early years education (including outdoor provision) can make a real difference to young children's outcomes and more so for those in 'vulnerable' groups. (p. 3)

Case Study Link

The relationship between play and learning out of doors is taken up in Chapter 6, Case Study 6.1.

Chapter Summary

- The legacies left to us by early philosophers and thinkers continue to inform the value we attach to play and how it underpins learning.
- Cognitive development is complex and requires a sound understanding of development in early childhood.
- Play in early childhood needs to be understood as a pedagogic approach.
- Academics and researchers working in the field of childhood have offered alternative and informative insights into children's early learning.
- Outdoor play is now recognised as an important element in early childhood learning.

Extended Reading

Brooker, L. Blaise, M. and Edwards, S. (2014) *The Sage Handbook of Play and Learning in Early Childhood*. London: Sage. A comprehensive and informative text that explores play and learning in detail and offers perspectives from a wide range of experts.

Izumi-Taylor, S. Pramling Samuelsson, I. and Rogers, C. S. (2010) 'Perspectives of play in three nations: a comparative study in Japan, the United States, and Sweden', *Early Childhood Research & Practice*, 12 (1): 1–12. An excellent and very readable article that offers contrasting accounts of play in the Early Years across three different nations and allows for comparison with the UK.

Mercer, J. (2018) *Child Development: Concepts and Theories*. London: Sage. A comprehensive and engaging text that is highly informative and examines the wider contexts within which child development occurs.

5
PRACTICE OUTSIDE OF THE MAINSTREAM

By the end of this chapter you should:

- appreciate that many approaches outside of the mainstream are highly effective
- know how to articulate the benefits that approaches outside of the mainstream can offer Early Years practitioners and teachers
- recognise the potential benefits that neuroscience can offer Early Years practitioners and teachers in primary schools
- understand the benefits and challenges that digital technology presents for Early Years practitioners and primary teachers

Loris Malaguzzi and Reggio Emilia

The Reggio Emilia approach evolved from the vision of Loris Malaguzzi (1920–1994), its original founder who was born in Corregio, in Italy. The approach has its origins in the small Italian town of Villa Cella when, following the end of World War II and the end of fascism, local people collected materials from destroyed buildings to build a school. Malaguzzi, who at the time was visiting the village, saw what was happening and decided to remain and work for the village, as a teacher. Whilst there is not a specifically defined approach, there are core principles with settings who follow the approach and develop in different ways. Children are viewed as unique individuals with an innate capacity to build their own knowledge of the world born out of a need to interact socially and being accorded the right to do so. Teachers are not trained to deliver one set curriculum, nor are they expected to work towards externally agreed targets, but rather they improve their teaching through developing their skills in observation and interpretation of children's behaviours.

Case Study Link

Key features of the Reggio Emilia approach are explored further in Chapter 6, Case Study 6.1.

Malaguzzi emphasised the importance of observation and clearly documenting aspects of children's learning; teachers do this by photographing the children whilst they learn and by making careful notes on their learning, as well as recording the verbal interactions of children when collaborating in group activities. Teachers meet weekly to share their observations and review their notes on each child's learning, which gives them opportunities to consider more fully the strengths and weaknesses of each child and to understand more fully their learning needs and learning styles. These meetings then support teachers with planning how to progress each child's learning and how they might shape learning activities in the forthcoming weeks; this process further enables them to achieve greater insights into the holistic needs of the children and their development.

Teachers as Partners in Learning

Teachers act as co-learners working alongside the children and facilitate learning through planning activities that focus on the interests of their pupils. Questioning is employed not only as a technique for improving children's comprehension but also as a means by which teachers can remain directly involved with their pupils as they learn; they listen closely to the children and document their learning using such tools as photographs of activities, drawings, children's work books, and so on. In doing so, they make learning and achievements more visible, thereby supporting the children in evaluating their own learning. Creative thinking is encouraged with specific attention being placed on problem-solving and exploration. Projects that take time are also encouraged as they give teachers opportunities to work alongside the children and get closely involved in their learning. Projects typically begin with teachers observing the children and questioning what is of particular interest to them; they then introduce materials to support learning and engage the children through further questioning, which shapes their projects and leads to further new projects.

> ### Critical Question
>
> Given the restrictions in social distancing brought about by COVID-19, what do you think the implications will be for teachers acting as co-learners and working alongside the children, and how might they address these?

A Hundred Languages

Malaguzzi (1998) employed the term 'hundred languages of children' to account for how children express their thinking; they are supported in this by teachers helping them to express their feelings. Children are supported in developing their thinking through the creative use of symbols, for example, drawing, sculpting and writing. Space and natural light are also seen as important, in addition to having indoor plants and ready access to the outdoors. Classrooms have spaces for social learning activities such as group collaborations, and the larger school environment is designed to give increased opportunities to interact with other children outside of the immediate classroom environment.

Discussion Point

If students were to have a placement in a Reggio Emilia setting how might this influence their thinking and practice, and to what extent might they then be able to implement features of this approach?

Te Whāriki

A celebrated approach to learning in early childhood, conceived originally in New Zealand in 1996 and then revised by the government in 2017, is the Te Whāriki approach; the philosophy underpinning this approach is at the heart of the curriculum promoted by the New Zealand government. Te Whāriki is not prescriptive; rather, it places great emphasis on the experiences and learning that children have in their own homes and communities, with happiness and wellbeing both viewed as extremely important. The approach views 'play' and 'communication' as central to learning and development in early childhood. Four key principles (MacBlain, 2018a) underpin the Te Whāriki approach (Table 5.1); as some words have different meanings and degrees of emphasis in the languages of Māori and English, texts outlining the approach contain words in both languages.

Table 5.1 Key principles of Te Whāriki approach

Principle	Description
Empowerment (in Māori – Whakamana)	Early years settings provide experiences where children are empowered to learn and develop socially and emotionally.
Holistic Development (in Māori – Kotahitanga)	Learning should address social and emotional factors, with these being central to holistic development.
Family and Community (in Māori – Whānau Tangata)	Family and community should be recognised as having a strong value in children's learning and development.
Relationships (in Māori – Ngā Hononga)	Positive relationships with others and with places and things are central to learning and development.

Source: Adapted from MacBlain (2018) p.85

In addition, the Te Whāriki approach (MacBlain, 2018) incorporates five key goals (Table 5.2).

Table 5.2 Key goals of the Te Whāriki approach

In Māori	Description
Mana Atua	The nurturing of children's health, including emotional health and wellbeing in situations where they can feel safe and secure.
Mana Whenua	Children and their families have a strong sense of belonging, with links to the wider societies in which they live that are valued and affirmed, and where they feel secure within the structures of these communities, the boundaries set and the customs that are integral to their communities.
Mana Tangata	Contribution where children are viewed as individuals and as equal, and their contributions valued, irrespective of background.
Mana Reo	Communication where practitioners encourage and facilitate children's own languages in addition to their cultures and the language, symbols, stories, and narratives of those cultures; non-verbal communication is also developed in addition to creativity and expression.
Mana Aotūroa	Children are encouraged to learn through exploring their environments; play is valued as a means of developing confidence and spontaneity in learning. Children learn to exercise control over their bodies and actions, learning strategies for problem-solving tasks which require them to think and apply logic, thereby helping them to make sense of their worlds.

Source: Adapted from MacBlain (2018) p.85

Some critics who themselves advocate holistic approaches to learning have expressed concerns about the difficulties in maintaining consistency across practice because learning outcomes have not been formally agreed, which can lead to significant variations in practice and in the setting of goals for individual children. Successive governments in New Zealand have acknowledged this criticism and there has been ongoing debate within government as to whether more formalised outcomes need to be embraced. It has been suggested, however, that this may lead to tensions between what were the intentions of the approach and what could become a more formalised system that imposes directives for practice and moves away from the original principles and aims of Te Whāriki.

> ### Activity
>
> View the following link: *Te Whariki – What is this Early Childhood 'Curriculum' that ECE Services are required by the Ministry of Education to follow?* My ECE Experts (© 2013–2017) Category: Teaching and Curriculum, available at: www.myece.org.nz/educational-curriculum-aspects/106-te-whariki-curriculum (accessed: 7 October 2020). Then, consider the relevance of this for Early Years practitioners and primary teachers in the UK.

Sure Start

Introduced in the UK in 1998, Sure Start had many of its origins in the 'Head Start' programme in the USA, developed in the 1960s to provide support for pre-school children from low-income families; it is of note that Bronfenbrenner, referred to in Chapter 3, was closely involved in the *Head Start* programme. Sure Start was designed to meet the needs of children from disadvantaged families in England; its popularity and high levels of success led to other areas of the UK such as Wales and Northern Ireland adopting and adapting the approach to suit their own communities, cultures, and particular needs. More specifically, Sure Start was designed to support children in having a better start in their lives, with improvements in child-care support for families being viewed as a core element of the approach; this in addition to supporting children's health and emotional wellbeing. Importantly, the approach also focused on supporting the development of communities that were characterised by disadvantage. When first introduced within the UK, the funding provided was significant, at £540 million between 1999 and 2002. At the time, it was estimated that around 150,000 young children in England were growing up in families and communities characterised by extreme deprivation.

Case Study Link

The impact of disadvantage on learning is explored in Chapters 7, 8, 9 and 10, in Case Studies 7.1, 8.1, 9.1 and 10.1, respectively.

An expectation placed on Sure Start children's centres was that they would provide a range of integrated services for their communities, bringing together external agencies working in relevant areas and all thereby benefiting from one another's expertise and experience and, in doing so, be able to offer multi-agency support for young children and their families. Though the government of the day agreed to allocate funding over a ten-year period, this in fact did not happen, and responsibility for funding and for overseeing the programme was moved to local authorities with the intention of setting up Sure Start centres in all communities. Since then, local authorities have shrunk considerably and are likely to continue to do so as the fallout from the global pandemic of 2020 takes a greater hold over their finances and the wider economy.

> ### Critical Question
>
> What factors today might suggest that government needs to offer greater financial support for pre-school children and their families living in areas of social deprivation?

Instrumental Enrichment

Over recent years there has emerged what I (the author) believe to be a truly enlightening approach to understanding, explaining and working with children that has its origins in the work of the celebrated psychologist Reuven Feuerstein (1921–2014). Feuerstein worked with children who survived the Holocaust following World War II; his experiences guided his thinking on how children, including those with severe and profound learning difficulties, think and learn. His experiences led him to develop his *Social Interactionist Theory*; in doing so, he explored how teachers perceive and act upon 'ability' in children as opposed to 'potential', and as a consequence he developed the approach known as *Dynamic Assessment*, where children are assessed over time on a range of activities using a number of 'instruments'. This approach to assessment contrasts markedly with that commonly used in formal education where children are assessed using standardised tests and the results then taken as a measure of their abilities as opposed to their potential.

Challenging Artificial Barriers

Feuerstein proposed that the belief systems we hold about children's learning should view potential as having no limits whilst acknowledging the existence of artificial barriers that can prevent children from realising their true potential. He further argued that all children, no matter what their degree of difficulty, can with appropriate support become effective learners. When this belief system is adopted by adults an enabling process takes place which supports children in learning how to learn, which extends throughout their lives (Burden, 1987). Feuerstein saw the key feature in learning how to learn as that of *Mediated Learning Experience*, and it is this feature that is central to his *Social Interactionist Theory* of learning. Feuerstein et al. (1980: 16) emphasised the importance of '...the way in which stimuli emitted by the environment are transferred by a 'mediating' agent, usually a parent, sibling, or other caregiver', and further emphasised how when mediated agents are guided by their '...intentions, culture, and emotional investment' they then select and organise '...the world of stimuli for the child', and by engaging in this process '...the cognitive structure of the child is affected'.

The key features of mediating learning are that:

- the mediator should be aware of, make known and ensure that the child has understood what is intended (*intentionality and reciprocity*)
- the mediator should explain why the child is going to work at a task (*investment of meaning*)
- the act should be viewed and understood as having value over and above the here and now (*transcendence*). (Burden, 1987).

Assessing Learning

Whilst Feuerstein emphasised the importance of 'dynamic' assessment as opposed to 'static' assessment, his ideas have sadly not been taken up by more Early Years practitioners and teachers. Assessing the learning of children as we have seen in previous chapters is a complicated affair, and too often judgements about children's abilities are formed on the back of tests given at a particular time and on a particular day which fail to assess underlying potential, and more especially fail to recognise artificial barriers to children's learning and academic progress. The concept of 'static' testing is charged with many problems, as indicated by Frederickson and Cline (2002):

> 'Static' tests such as IQ tests evaluate what a child has learned in the past – their zone of actual development... It is seen as more useful to assess what Vygotsky called the zone of proximal development... For this purpose 'dynamic' measures are required... static tests... establish current levels of performance but usually tell us little about the processes that underlie that competence (Campione, 1989). They ignore functions that have not yet matured... (pp. 252–3)

Discussion Point

How useful is 'static' assessment in recording children's learning in the Early Years?

The Contribution of Neuroscience

It is becoming more and more accepted that the field of neuroscience has much to offer when it comes to understanding broader social, emotional, and cognitive learning in childhood, and, as new research emerges, we are building a better and more accurate picture of how and why children learn in unique and individual ways (MacBlain, 2014; Whitebread, 2012). This is perhaps one of the most exciting fields in early learning.

Early learning allows us to develop the skills we need for later life

Brain Development and Learning in Early Childhood

To fully appreciate how brain development impacts on learning in early childhood we need to understand the important role that neurons play. It is through neurons that information passes within the brain in the form of electrical impulses, with estimations of the number of neurons in the brain being in the region of many billions. As the foetus develops prior to birth, neurons are already forming in different parts of the brain, and as they do, they establish responses to different chemicals. The process starts in the more primitive areas of the brain, for example, the brainstem where the autonomic functions that will be necessary for bodily development lie. By the time children are born these functions are relatively well developed, and therefore new-born infants can take nourishment by sucking; they are also able to breathe and can sleep and hear sounds and experience other sensations such as touch. Following birth, more advanced areas of the infant's brain develop, for example, the cerebral cortex, which allows for the development of more advanced functioning such as the development of language and thinking. Different areas of the brain develop their own functions through chemical agents known as *hormones* and *neurotransmitters*.

Neurons do not make direct contact with each other; instead, there are tiny spaces or gaps between them known as *synapses* across which impulses travel, and as this occurs chemicals are released known as *transmitter substances*. Synapses develop at an extraordinary rate in new-born infants and during early childhood. Whilst many synapses become established, others do not and are abandoned, and this process continues throughout the lives of individuals; by adolescence it is estimated that around half of an individual's synapses have been abandoned (MacBlain, 2014).

A further and important process that is happening in early brain development is *myelination*. A 'fatty' substance known as myelin acts as an insulator and facilitates the transmission of impulses across synapses. It is important to note that the type of experiences and the level of stimulation given to infants and young children in their first months and years impacts on the development of myelination and later learning. As experiences are encountered by children and then repeated, the sensory neural pathways that are being established in the brain contribute to the construction of memories; in this way the brain supports the developing child in adapting to their environment and constructing their understanding of the world in which they are growing up. By the time young children reach the age when they attend pre-school, their brains are almost fully grown. The importance of the genetic make-up inherited by children and its interrelationship with how children experience their environments is also now much better understood.

Digital Learning in Early Childhood

Digital Challenges in the 21st Century

A further exciting field in early learning that is producing some wonderful research is that of digital learning. Digital learning can be said to be challenging much traditional mainstream thinking and practice in ways that are yet to be understood. Indeed, it can be argued that the educational landscape in Early Years practice and teaching is changing at a rate unprecedented in history. Thinking outside mainstream practice increasingly challenges practitioners and teachers to look closely at the unfolding and ever-accelerating pace at which digital technology is now impacting on learning in childhood. Recently, Carr and Lee (2019) commented, regarding practice in New Zealand, how:

> Today, some centres provide Learning Stories online, and families access them by mobile phone or computer and are able to send them on to families who live at a distance. ICT is now a valued integral part of the communication with families… (p. 129)

Almost everywhere we look we see children engaging with digital technology. Even children in their first years typically have access to smart phones, computers, and a variety of digital devices in their homes (Teichert and Anderson, 2014); many pre-school children can now be observed using digital tablet devices. Some years ago, ChildWise (2015) estimated that nearly a half of children in the UK use these every day. Indeed, many young children now use tablet computers almost as second nature and it is not uncommon to see even toddlers swiping the screens of their parents' smart phones to play games and watch videos, send messages and make video calls, a practice that is generally permitted and often encouraged by parents and has been increasingly used by families during the recent COVID-19 pandemic, when the only way many families can see each other is using apps such as Zoom, Skype and so on.

Learning through digital technology can be a shared experience enjoyed by all the family

Most children starting in Early Years settings will already have had access to digital technology at home. Neumann and Neumann (2014) have emphasised how tablet computers emulate features of books and, in doing so, offer children exciting and worthwhile opportunities to develop their literacy skills and knowledge whilst also developing their confidence and skills in using technology. Many apps are now designed to support children with creating their own stories, which can include pictures and even sounds; this makes them more appealing and can motivate children to engage much more with reading (Kucirkova and Sakr, 2015). Over recent decades parents have increasingly invested in digital technology in the belief that their investment will add value to their children's learning and educational progress. In some instances, ownership of the latest digital technology may even be seen as a sign of good parenting (Willett, 2015). Carr and Lee (2019) have also emphasised how, for example, e-portfolios '…have a distinct place in providing families with immediate access', to children's learning, thereby 'enabling learning interests and activities to be connected across the "borders" between home and school stories' (p. 131).

Some years ago, the Office for National Statistics ONS (2015), looking at mental health and wellbeing in children in the UK, noted how those children who spend more than three hours per day on social media sites were more than twice as likely to have poor mental health. Another area of concern that can impact significantly on learning in early childhood is cyber bullying. This is, as yet, an aspect of digital learning that is not properly understood and that needs far greater clarity through focused and purposeful research in the field. Again, it is worth considering, given the fact that many children who have not been attending Early Years and primary settings because of COVID-19 may have been spending much greater periods of time at computers – and in some cases excessive amounts of time – if this too is an issue that needs greater research.

Critical Question

How might digital technologies be used to support early learning at a time when practitioners and teachers are having to manage the challenges brought about by COVID-19?

Chapter Summary

- There are many approaches to learning in early childhood that lie outside of the mainstream and that have proven to be highly effective.
- Taking time to consider and reflect on how others have approached learning in early childhood can be extremely valuable and can impact hugely on one's own practice.
- Being able to articulate the key elements of practice outside of the mainstream can add significantly to how adults working with young children are able to engage in meaningful dialogue with other professionals and parents.
- One emerging field that is offering rich and exciting insights into how young children learn is neuroscience.
- Today's practitioners and teachers face exciting challenges that are accelerating as children increasingly engage with digital technology and social media.
- Within the UK there is a high level of inspection and accountability, and adults working with young children are increasingly expected to account for why they practice in particular ways and not in others.

Extended Reading

Carr, M. and Lee, W. (2019) *Learning Stories in Practice*. London: Sage. An accessible and visual text that explores many aspects of learning in early childhood, drawing particularly on practice in New Zealand.

Conkbayir, M. (2017) *Early Childhood and Neuroscience*. London: Bloomsbury. A most interesting and accessible text, which explores the contributions of neuroscience to learning and development in early childhood.

Murata, K. (2014) *[New Zealand] Overview and Recent Issues of New Zealand Early Childhood Education Curriculum (Te Whāriki)*. Available at www.childresearch.net/projects/ecec/2014_04.html (accessed: 3 October 2020). An excellent and comprehensive account of Te Whāriki and recent issues that have presented themselves with this approach.

PART THREE

SEEING THEORY IN PRACTICE

6: Play as a Pedagogic Approach
7: Emotional Learning in Early Childhood
8: Social Learning in Early Childhood
9: Language and Learning
10: Health and Wellbeing

Part Three offers nine case studies designed to illustrate how theory can be applied to practice. Chapter 6 explores, through Case Study 6.1, the importance of understanding play as a pedagogic approach and how it is central to learning in early childhood. Chapter 7 then introduces us to 'Robbie, Pradeep and Gita' in Case Study 7.1, and follows their development and learning from birth to Key Stage 2 through subsequent chapters in Case Study 8.1, Case Study 9.1, and Case Study 10.1. Chapters 7 to 10 also offer the following additional cases: Case Study 7.2, Case Study 8.2, Case Study 9.2 and Case Study 10.2, which focus on: emotional development and learning; social development and learning; language and learning; and health and wellbeing.

6
PLAY AS A PEDAGOGIC APPROACH

Perhaps above all, play is a simple joy that is a cherished part of childhood.

(Ginsberg et al., 2007: 183)

By the end of this chapter you should:

- appreciate how the outdoor environment and changing weather can be used to support new as well as prior learning
- recognise the quality of learning that can take place out of doors
- have gained insights into activities that support learning out of doors
- be clear about play as a pedagogic approach
- appreciate the wonderful and complex aspects of learning that children can engage in when afforded opportunities to play out of doors

Play is central to learning in early childhood, and though this has been recognised by early pioneers and most theorists for generations there remain those who fail to fully recognise the extent to which play in early childhood is inseparable from learning. There are even some who, despite the evidence produced by academics and practitioners, view play in Early Years settings as an unnecessary distraction from learning. Case Study 6.1 explores how a recent fall of snow provides exciting opportunities for new learning as well as opportunities to consolidate prior learning in an Early Years setting. This Case Study also challenges us to consider the potential that practice outside of the mainstream can offer Early Years practitioners and teachers.

Learning through play is key to intellectual development

Case Study 6.1: Play as Pedagogy: Learning Out of Doors

Changes in the weather are seen by staff at Little Ones nursery as providing excellent opportunities for new learning as well as consolidating prior learning. During the summer the children make and float little boats outside with the help of staff, when it is windy they make and fly kites, when it rains they splash in puddles, and during autumn they collect and make patterns with leaves. It is now winter, and snow has been forecast for the following day. After all the children have been collected the staff meet and plan the activities for the following day when everywhere outside will be covered in snow; they plant containers outside with water that will freeze and provide opportunities for the children to discover frozen water and experience 'slippery' surfaces that 'sparkle' in the sunshine. The children arrive at school on the following day and as the sun comes out, they are helped to dress in warm clothes, with hats, scarves, and gloves; earlier that morning two staff have already been outside and built a snowman. Once outside the children are left to begin touching the snow and ice, running their fingers and hands through and along it, making marks, patterns and shapes and comparing these with those made by their friends and even making letters if they are able – some can even write their own name. As they play and learn, the adults provide words to describe this new and exciting environment, *'frosty'*, *'snowy'*, *'sparkling'*, *'crackly'*, which will add to the children's vocabularies. As the children move around independently they discover spoons left outside the previous evening by staff, which act as tools and that enable them to make shapes and patterns in the snow and on the ice and even shape letters and words they have learned, which will reinforce previous writing activities. As the children move around, some staff begin singing *'we are looking for lots of interesting shapes in the ice and snow and we are not cold'* and the children are encouraged to join in. The children work with others to find new shapes and patterns, which staff then discuss with them, naming some of the shapes as 'square', 'circle', 'long', 'short', and so on. The session also offers opportunities to support the children in seeing how snow changes and melts and to introduce the children to concepts such as 'freezing' and 'melting'. Staff motivate the children with their own curiosity, and through their own excited responses model positive thinking skills by asking such questions as 'What if I did this…?' 'I wonder how…?' and 'What makes this happen like this…?' and so on. Back indoors the children now work in small groups with an adult; on each table is a small bowl with some pieces of ice that have been collected, together with some food dye of different colours. Using pipettes, the children suck up some of the dye and then drop it onto the ice and watch as the ice changes colour. When they add new colours they see how the original colours change. Staff also introduce the children to new words such as 'dye', 'redden', 'freezing', 'purple', 'melting', 'chilly', 'frozen' and 'wintry'. This activity is followed by a story about a snowman and after lunch the children are asked to collaborate verbally by sharing what they enjoyed doing best in the snow.

> ### Critical Question
>
> What considerations would staff in Case Study 6.1 have made before taking the children outside and how would these be different now, given that Early Years settings have to manage social distancing because of COVID-19?

Signposts to Theory

It is clear from Case Study 6.1 that the children are actively engaging in emotional and social learning, in addition to developing their intellectual skills and cognitive abilities; they are doing this by exploring this new and exciting environment, collaborating with their peers and with the adults and sharing their excitement through language, and through their actions. Here we are reminded of how Fontana (1995), cited earlier in the Introduction, described learning as '...not something that happens to individuals... but something which they themselves make happen by the manner in which they handle incoming information and put it to use' (p. 145). This is clearly the approach that is being taken by staff at the nursery; learning is not happening to the children but rather, they are making learning happen as they 'handle incoming information and put it to use'. Such an approach is very much in contrast to that offered to young children decades ago who, in line with a *behaviourist* approach, were made to sit quietly and follow instructions with their learning being something that *'happens'* to them. Each of the theoretical approaches covered in Part Two would support the principles guiding staff at the nursery, and it is clear that there is an abundance of highly creative learning opportunities being created for the children; they are also being introduced to purposeful and meaningful learning opportunities that allow staff to observe and informally assess their individual learning.

We saw in Chapter 1 how the early pioneers valued freedom in childhood and the absence of over-control; here, in contrast to being overly directed in their learning, the children are encouraged to explore, which is also in keeping with the theoretical approaches of Piaget and Bruner, who emphasised the importance of children acting upon their environments and thereby constructing new understandings and internalising and accommodating new knowledge. Ginsberg et al. (2007) have drawn attention to how much of children's play in early childhood will include adults. In some instances, adults can become overly involved and controlling of children's learning, which can mean that '...children acquiesce to adult rules and concerns and lose some of the benefits play offers them, particularly in developing creativity, leadership, and group skills...' (p. 183).

The children's social language is also being developed in accordance with the theoretical approaches offered by other theorists such as Bandura and Vygotsky who emphasised the importance of learning as a social activity. Importantly, the children are also engaging in learning as part of their community, which is in line with the ideas offered by Rogoff explored in Chapter 3. Other approaches such as those of Isaacs and Dewey, which emphasised the emotional side of young children's learning, are also in keeping with what staff at the nursery are doing. It is also evident that staff have been inspired by the ideas of the Reggio Emelia approach that was discussed in Chapter 5 as evidenced by their use of *'provocations'*, which are different to *'invitations'*. *Provocations* have been explained by The Compass School (2019) as 'an experience set up in response to a child's interests and ideas', and *invitations* as 'a more direct piece of encouragement for exploration'. We saw how the Reggio Emelia approach places significant emphasis on learning through action, which is central to the thinking of staff in Case Study 6.1. Here, we can also observe some similarities to the ideas of Piaget, who emphasised that children actively engaging with their environment is key to their learning. We can also draw some tenuous links to the *behaviourist* approach and more particularly *operant conditioning* discussed in Chapter 3, where children are rewarded after initiating an action, thereby leading potentially to a reinforcement of that action or pattern of behaviours.

> ### Critical Question
>
> What aspects of the children's learning in Case Study 6.1 are being reinforced and how might this be explained by *behaviourist* theory?

Nature provides wonderful resources for early learning

In addition to their cognitive and intellectual development being supported, the children are also developing their physical and emotional skills. As the children engage in learning within their new snow-covered environment, they are enhancing their confidence and resilience as they face new and exciting challenges. This is a point emphasised by Ginsberg et al. (2007), who noted the importance of play in promoting healthy child development and supporting emotional learning, as follows: '…play helps children develop new competencies that lead to enhanced confidence and the resiliency they will need to face future challenges' (p. 183). Ginsberg et al. also articulated the social nature of play, which 'allows children to learn how to work in groups, to share, to negotiate, to resolve conflicts, and to learn self-advocacy skills...' (p. 183). This is of course in keeping with the theoretical approaches offered by Bandura and Vygotsky, both of whom emphasised the social nature of learning and how social interaction through play not only supports intellectual development – as, for example, with reasoning and logical thinking – but importantly also the development of self-confidence and self-esteem. We saw in Chapter 3 the importance of self-efficacy and how this contributes to children's social learning and provides a sound basis for later more formal learning. Case Study 6.1 clearly indicates how the children are actively engaging socially with their peers and adults, both through their physical actions and through language.

Within the nursery some children will be less advanced in their language than others, and therefore being able to learn out of doors in the snow will support them in using their language to communicate with the other children. Importantly, Ginsberg et al. have drawn attention to some of the benefits that play has for children who are less verbal and who find it difficult to mix with their peers: 'Less verbal children may be able to express their views, experiences, and even frustrations through play' (2007: 183). It is of note that the adults are introducing the children to new vocabulary and then, as a behaviourist approach would indicate, reinforcing the learning of new words back indoors when the children return inside.

Ginsberg et al. have also drawn attention to the way in which play needs to be accepted as being central to more formal learning when children first begin school, as play '...has been shown to help children adjust to the school setting and even to enhance children's learning readiness, learning behaviors, and problem-solving skills', and they have emphasised how 'social-emotional learning is best integrated with academic learning' (2007: 183). When we think of the above case we can find meaning in the ideas of Vygotsky (Chapter 3) who viewed play as being extremely important in children's learning, proposing that through play young children come to develop their understanding of the different relationships they have with others.

Case Study 6.1 also recognises the importance of adult-supported learning, where adults are working alongside the children and supporting their actions and learning as opposed to simply directing their learning; such a view falls within the scope of many of the theoretical perspectives explored in Part Two, for example, that of Vygotsky and Bruner and the notion of 'scaffolding'. The ideas offered by Feuerstein in Chapter 5 are also relevant, and readers will see how the adults working with the children in Case Study 6.1 were in many ways 'mediating' their learning.

Chapter Link

Revisit the ideas offered by Feuerstein in Chapter 5 and the concept of 'mediated' learning.

Activity

Access the following link: DfE (2017) – Authors: Callanan, M., Anderson, M., Haywood, S., Hudson, R. and Speight, S. *Social Research Study of Early Education and Development: Good Practice in Early Education Research Report*, NatCen, available at: https://assets.publishing.service.gov.uk/government/uploads/system/uploads/attachment_data/file/586242/SEED__Good_Practice_in_Early_Education_-_RR553.pdf (accessed: 16 August 2019).

Look particularly at the section 'Views on what works in supporting children's learning and development' (p. 9) and identify key factors that support best practice in early learning.

Extended Reading

Burnett, C., Daniels, K. and Sawka, V. (2016), 'Teaching strategies', in D. Wyse and S. Rogers (2016) (eds), *A Guide to Early Years & Primary Teaching*. London: Sage. An excellent chapter that offers rich insights into the opportunities that play can offer Early Years practitioners and teachers in primary schools.

Maynard, T. and Waters, J. (2007) 'Learning in the outdoor environment: a missed opportunity?' *Early Years*, 27: 255–65. An insightful article on the potential that learning out of doors offers children in early childhood.

Sackville-Ford, M. and Davenport, H. (eds) (2019) *Critical Issues in Forest Schools*. London: Sage. An in-depth look at the concept of 'Forest Schools' with contributions from experts in the field.

7

EMOTIONAL LEARNING IN EARLY CHILDHOOD

By the end of this chapter you should:

- understand how the quality of experiences in the weeks and months following birth impact on emotional learning
- appreciate how early experiences are important foundations for later development and learning
- understand the importance of strong self-efficacy and how this underpins emotional development and learning throughout childhood
- have a better understanding of behaviour modification, which is central to *behaviourist* theory
- appreciate the challenges faced by many students on placement in Early Years settings and primary schools when working on an individual basis with children

Case Study 7.1: Life Begins for Robbie, Pradeep, and Gita

Robbie, Pradeep, and Gita are all born in the same year, in the same town and in the same hospital, and will attend the same nursery and primary school; following birth they share the same Health Visitor. At birth, Robbie's family is already known to Social Services as both of his parents are registered Class A drug users, in addition to being alcohol dependent. When Robbie is only a few weeks old the Health Visitor contacts Social Services expressing concerns about Robbie's home environment and absence of positive care, as well as contacting the local paediatrician about her fears for Robbie's general development. Unlike Robbie, Pradeep is born quite prematurely to parents who are devoted to him; the Health Visitor observes over the coming months that some aspects of Pradeep's development appear slower than expected, though she is not overly concerned by this. Like Pradeep, Gita is also born to devoted parents and in the following months the Health Visitor notes how Gita enjoys interacting with everyone around her. She also notes that Gita's language is developing well and that she is a very contented child, evidenced by her willingness to engage with others. From birth, Pradeep and Gita's parents establish routines with feeding and sleeping, which contrasts with Robbie's parents who do not establish routines and respond to Robbie only when it suits them.

Critical Question

When and how might Early Years practitioners work with Health Visitors?

Signposts to Theory

Though Robbie, Pradeep and Gita are at the same stage, the features of this stage and how they might move through it have been explained differently by theorists, as we saw in Part One (see Tables 7.1 and 7.2).

Table 7.1 Contrasting explanations

Stage	Key features
Sensorimotor (Piaget)	Children learn through their senses and motor abilities, and by trial and error, which prepares them for the next stage.
Oral (Freud)	Children derive satisfaction from putting things in their mouths, which meets the needs of the libido.
Trust versus mistrust (Erikson)	Children are developing a sense of trust in the world around them, which is dependent upon consistency and reliability.

Table 7.2 Progression through stages

Stage	Successful	Unsuccessful
Sensorimotor (Piaget)	Children learn to adapt meaningfully to the world.	Intellectual foundations for next stage not established.
Oral (Freud)	Children develop a greater sense of security.	Children can develop fixations in later life, e.g. thumb-sucking, which increase with anxiety.
Trust versus mistrust (Erikson)	Strong sense of security with quality of care received being taken into future relationships.	Children carry mistrust into future relationships with associated anxieties.

Early bonding is a natural process and lays the foundations for later security and learning

Drawing on Piaget's approach all three children are now moving through the *sensorimotor* stage when infants learn through their senses. If, on the other hand, we draw on Freud's *psychodynamic* theory we can see that they are in the *oral* stage, which, according to this approach, can give us some insights into possible future personality development. Given that Robbie is already experiencing significant difficulties with emotional attachment then this approach would suggest that he may face problems later in life because the needs of his libido are not being satisfied due to the lack of emotional bonding with his parents. If we look to Erikson's theory we can see that it is likely Robbie will carry a strong sense of mistrust into his future relationships accompanied by higher levels of anxiety, whilst Pradeep and Gita will have already been internalising high levels of quality in their own care, which Erikson's theory suggests they will take into future relationships.

We know that children during this stage are quite helpless, though the level of helplessness experienced by Robbie is clearly far greater than that experienced by Pradeep and Gita due to the lack of consistency and empathy shown to him by his parents. Some years ago, Pearce (2009) captured the crucial role that primary caregivers need to play in managing helplessness by nurturing new-born infants and establishing routines early on, something that has been absent in Robbie's early life:

> When children are born they... are innately endowed with the capacity to call attention to their fundamental needs, but do not have the capacity to satisfy their needs themselves. They rely on adults to do so... The maintenance of routines is a sense of comfort and reassurance to the child as it facilitates an understanding of the predictability of events and the behaviour and responsiveness of others. (p. 59)

It is clear that in the case of Robbie all of the factors identified by Pearce are missing in his early life, for example, routines around feeding and sleeping, which are in stark contrast to those of Pradeep and Gita whose parents established feeding and sleeping routines soon after birth, thereby giving them a sense of stability, continuity and security, which will support them later with their learning. Given the lack of stability and positive care in Robbie's early life and especially his poor emotional attachment to both parents, it is very probable, according to Freud's *psychodynamic* approach, that Robbie will experience significant difficulties in forming secure relationships later in his childhood and perhaps, most worryingly, in adulthood when he himself becomes a parent.

Robbie has been born into a family where he is being deprived of those important elements described by Pearce and emphasised by others such as John Bowlby and Mary Ainsworth that many take for granted and that have their basis in being loved. The importance of love in early childhood and its influence on learning cannot be over-emphasised; though well-understood even by the early pioneers, this core feature of emotional development has not always been accorded the prominence it deserves. The importance of love in early childhood and its potential impact on emotional development and therefore learning has been wonderfully articulated by Curran (2012), as follows:

> IT IS EXTRAORDINARY TO ME that in the last 15 years of brain research, all those billions of dollars spent in laboratories has shown to me one single important message. It can best be set out as follows... If a child is in an environment where they are *understood* as an individual human being then... Their *self-esteem* will be improved, and... If their self-esteem is good they will gain *self-confidence*... If they are in an environment where their self-esteem is good and they have self-confidence, they will feel *engaged* with that environment. And what does all that add up to? Well, love as it happens. (p. 5)

Being loved as a child offers children stability and consistency in their lives and provides important foundations for later emotional, social, and cognitive development and learning.

If we turn to the *behaviourist* approach to help us further with understanding Robbie's emotional development and how this will impact on later learning, we need first to revisit what is a core tenet of *behaviourist* theory, that 'all behaviour is learned' and 'all actions have consequences'. Unlike Pradeep and Gita who receive regular positive reinforcement of desired behaviours from their parents, Robbie is continually exposed to negative reinforcement and even at such an early level of development is already being conditioned to form associations between behaviours such as crying and negative consequences from his parents such as being shouted at or ignored; as an infant he is learning to associate at a subconscious level his cries for attention with neglect and aggression.

When we apply the *behaviourist* principles of *operant conditioning* discussed in Chapter 3 we can see that when Robbie behaves in particular ways, he experiences negative consequences, which through association are not only impacting on his emotional development and wellbeing but will also come to impact later on in how he thinks about himself, his self-esteem and his abilities or self-efficacy, which Bandura emphasised in his theory of *Social Learning* as being central to learning. In contrast to Robbie, Pradeep and Gita are receiving constant reinforcement through positive affirmation of their actions and behaviours, which will lead to increased positive self-esteem and strong self-efficacy.

The Children's Social Learning

When we consider the learning experiences of Robbie, Pradeep, and Gita outside of the home it is helpful to explore how wider influences are impacting on them. Here, Bronfenbrenner's *Ecological Theory* discussed in Chapter 3 can be helpful. We can, for example, explain aspects of Robbie's development in terms of the limited opportunities he has had at the *microsystem* level when as a child he is being given very limited opportunities to form significant and positive relationships with other adults and children outside of his home. At the *mesosystem* level Robbie may have experienced some positive connections outside of his home such as playgroup or wider family members, but these will have been very limited and much in contrast to Pradeep and Gita whose parents are very sociable and have taken them to different playgroups and activities to meet with others in a wide variety of social settings. At the *exosystem* level his experiences will also have been very limited as his mother and father rarely leave their home other than to go drinking with dubious friends or take Robbie to the local supermarket to buy groceries and provisions for the home. At the *chronosystem* level the sum of Robbie's experiences as the months have gone by have, unlike those of Pradeep and Gita, been extremely limited.

Confidence in one's ability to learn begins with those first actions

Case Study 7.2: Promoting Self-Efficacy

Angela has just begun her student placement in a Year 1 class at the local primary school and has been asked to observe and work with three children, Dick, Shane, and Esme. She quickly notices how when Dick and Shane are asked to work with other children in group activities, they appear very reluctant and even anxious, preferring instead to work individually by themselves. As the days pass, Angela notes how they rarely initiate conversations with other children and become quickly bored with most activities, moving constantly from one thing to another without sustaining concentration even for a limited time. She also observes how they spend a lot of time watching the other children but never join them. In contrast, Esme is quick to engage with other children and to readily offer suggestions and put forward her own ideas. Angela notes particularly how enthusiastic Esme is when asked to work with other children. Angela decides that she will employ some of the principles of *behaviourism* that she has learned on her course. That night, she buys a large bag of coloured marbles which she takes into the classroom the next day along with two large jam jars. She shows Dick and Shane the marbles and tells them that she is going to ask them to attempt a number of tasks, which if they complete will win them a marble that they can put in their jar; the two boys become very excited and even more so when Angela tells them that when each jar is full they will receive a smiley face sticker to put on the class chart. On the following day Angela asks the two boys to attempt and finish a task; they quickly do so, and she then gives them each a marble to put in their jar. Angela repeats this process each day, though each time she makes the task a little more difficult. Over the coming days she observes how both boys are keen to complete the tasks even though they are getting harder. After a fortnight both jars are full, and the boys are given a smiley face sticker for the class chart; they are delighted! Angela notes how tasks that would have given them a challenge previously, and that they would have avoided, have in fact become more enjoyable to them. She decides as the days go by to further develop this *behaviourist* approach and decides to implement the principles of *operant conditioning*, which she has also learned about on her course. To do this, she carefully observes the two boys and when they become actively engaged in working on a task, she goes over to them and smiles and offers some words of encouragement; the children look at her and smile back. Angela repeats this several times as the children engage with different parts of the task and she notices that after she has smiled and praised them, they engage with greater enthusiasm with what they are doing. She continues this approach over the following weeks and notices how both boys are developing in self-confidence as evidenced by their increased willingness to attempt tasks they would have previously avoided. By the end of her placement, Angela has noted a significant change in the boys' behaviours, just as she had hoped for, given her application of the principles of *operant conditioning*.

Critical Question

What can Early Years practitioners and teachers in primary schools do to develop self-efficacy in children from dysfunctional families?

Signposts to Theory

Bandura's theory of *Social Learning* that was discussed in Chapter 3 can help us understand and explain Dick and Shane's apparent lack of belief in their ability to engage with activities they think are challenging, and provides us with a framework for interpreting and understanding the self-efficacy of both boys. This approach suggests that even at such a young age Dick and Shane have already internalised thinking processes that indicate low-self-efficacy and that are often seen in older children with low self-esteem and weak self-efficacy. Both boys avoid tasks that they see as challenging and have already acquired a strong tendency to focus on the negative as opposed to thinking they could at least attempt tasks that appear difficult. Bandura's theory also helps us explain why Dick and Shane have internalised patterns of thinking that are irrational and cause them to believe they will be unsuccessful with tasks that are unfamiliar to them and appear difficult. We can hypothesise with some degree of certainty that, unlike Esme, Dick and Shane will have had adverse experiences in early childhood and emotionally impoverished relationships in their first years.

Drawing upon Bandura's work we can also hypothesise that Dick and Shane could improve their self-efficacy by observing other more confident children and adults and imitating how they approach tasks that are challenging. We know that whilst self-efficacy cannot be taught there are many things adults can do to strengthen it in children. Bandura suggested, for example, that this can be done by adults supporting children in developing a sense of 'mastery' through such activities as observing other children with high levels of self-efficacy, engaging with challenges whilst being supported by an adult and receiving regular affirmation in the form of verbal comments from significant adults, which also fits with a *behaviourist* approach where positive reinforcement through regular affirmation of desired behaviours strengthens self-esteem and, as indicated by Feuerstein in Chapter 5, supports children in learning how to learn. Importantly, Bandura emphasised that children with weak self-efficacy should be supported in gaining a better understanding of their emotions and feelings as these arise; this is an approach that was clearly used by Angela who had observed at the end of her placement how Dick and Shane's self-esteem and confidence had improved.

> ## Chapter Link
>
> Chapter 2 offers further details on how self-efficacy can be improved by teachers.

We also saw in Chapter 3 how Bandura, cited in Hayes (1994: 477), had identified four psychological processes that were heavily influenced by the self-efficacy beliefs of individuals, outlined below in Table 7.3

Table 7.3 Bandura's psychological processes that influence self-efficacy

Cognitive	Faced with challenges children reflect initially on whether they can succeed, then direct their thinking towards managing the challenge.
Motivational	Highly motivated children apply themselves with excitement and persistence. Those with limited motivation give up all too readily.
Affective	Children with low self-efficacy can experience higher levels of anxiety when asked to complete activities they see as difficult.
Selection	Young children attempt challenges as they view them within their capability. Those with weak self-efficacy typically avoid them.

Taking each of the processes in Table 7.3 in turn we note that in regard to their cognitive development, all three children are of similar intellectual ability. Applying Piagetian theory, this would place them in the *preoperational* stage and more specifically the second sub-stage, *intuitive* (4–7 years), when children's developing cognitive abilities allow them to reflect more on whole situations as opposed to focusing, as younger children do, on detail. Here, we can also draw on Bruner's theoretical approach discussed in Chapter 4, which proposed that children represent their worlds through three modes, *enactive*, *iconic*, and *symbolic*, that link to the nature of children's life experiences; this point is important as it causes us to reflect on the life experiences of Dick and Shane and Esme prior to starting primary school. All three children will have developed their intellectual capacity within the *enactive mode* when as new-born infants their view of objects was connected to their physical movements. Their intellectual abilities would also have been served by the *iconic mode* when children represent objects as images, thereby allowing them to advance their cognitive abilities through thinking of objects and people not immediately present in their environment. This mode, it must be remembered, is limiting in that children do not have the cognitive capacity to represent and store abstract concepts such as sadness and happiness in their brains. By Year 1, the children would have been functioning in Bruner's final mode, *symbolic*, when through their language skills they can store abstract concepts, though their immaturity and early language development would place limits on their intellectual functioning. It is worth recalling the excellent example offered by Brown (1977), which illustrates so well children's thinking in this final mode and explains how it differs from the *iconic* mode:

> A photograph or a model of a cow would be an icon in that it would represent the animal in a very real and obvious way. The symbols C-O-W have no such characteristics. They only signify the existence of the animal by consensus of those who use the word. (p. 74)

The children's development in language will have increasingly helped them to communicate verbally with others in an abstract way, allowing them to join in problem-solving activities with other children and in reflection.

With the second of Bandura's processes in Table 7.3, *motivational*, we can see that whilst Esme is highly motivated and applies herself wholeheartedly to learning situations that present challenges and persists in her attempts to see these through to completion, Dick and Shane have little motivation and give up all too readily when presented with a challenge. If we take Bandura's third process, *affective*, we can reflect on how anxiety may have affected how the boys approached new learning situations; asked to engage in activities that presented a challenge both boys would have experienced higher levels of stress than Esme. Bandura's final process, *selection*, helps us understand that the boys would have been limited in their selection of tasks, whereas Esme would try anything because her self-efficacy is much stronger.

If we look to *behaviourist* theory, we can see that Angela employed 'behaviour modification' to shape the boys' behaviours, and, in doing so, also shaped how they approached increasingly difficult tasks over the coming weeks. In effect, she was not trying to explain to the boys why they should attempt difficult tasks; instead, she was shaping their learning through extinguishing previously learned behaviour patterns and replacing these with new ones through a process of reinforcement. Angela was also employing *operant conditioning* as another powerful *behaviourist* technique; to do this, she waited until the children initiated a desired learning behaviour such as attempting a difficult task and then went to them and praised them; importantly, the praise came after the boys initiated the desired behaviour.

Discussion Point

Why should the children's teacher be guarded against judging Esme to be more intellectually able than the two boys? How could she assess the boys' true intellectual capacity?

Extended Reading

Aubrey, K. and Riley, A. (2017) *Understanding & Using Challenging Educational Theories*. London: Sage. A comprehensive text that examines theoretical approaches which have challenged thinking and practice over past decades.

Cowie, H. (2012) *From Birth to Sixteen: Children's Health, Social, Emotional and Linguistic Development*. London: Routledge. An informative text that looks at early development and the impact of social, emotional, and cognitive experiences in later childhood and adolescence.

Pearce, C. (2009) *A Short Introduction to Attachment and Attachment Disorder*. London: Jessica Kingsley. This text explains attachment and attachment disorder thoroughly and addresses its impact on child development.

8

SOCIAL LEARNING IN EARLY CHILDHOOD

By the end of this chapter you should:

- recognise how development in the first years influences early as well as later learning
- understand how early social learning lays down important foundations for future emotional and cognitive growth and academic achievement
- be clear as to why accurate assessment is important
- know why Early Years practitioners and teachers need to exercise caution when formally recording and reporting outcomes based on their observations of children's behaviours and test results.
- recognise the contribution that *Attribution Theory* can make
- understand the importance of teaching children strategies for learning that are effective and individual to their needs

Case Study 8.1: Robbie, Pradeep, and Gita Start Nursery

All three children are now two and a half years of age and attending nursery school. Robbie is noticeably smaller in stature than the others, and unlike Pradeep and Gita who quickly run to meet the other children and key staff, Robbie cries inconsolably when left by either of his parents. His language is noticeably delayed, and he struggles to express himself having only a few intelligible words. Robbie often arrives late to nursery wearing a nappy, unwashed and in dirty clothes. He cries uncontrollably when his mother or father leave him and then constantly seeks reassurance from staff and to be held and given cuddles. The nursery staff note that '*when he is with his parents he displays contradictory behaviour patterns such as wanting to be close to his parents but making little eye contact with them, approaching his parents but stopping and staring before making physical contact and engaging and disengaging with them simultaneously*'. Robbie regularly hits other children and on occasions swears at staff when checked. In contrast, Pradeep and Gita are well behaved, enjoy mixing and playing with their peers and present as confident, articulate, and able children. Pradeep is described by staff as '*a delightful child though very clumsy and quite immature*' and '*always bumping into things and seems to fall over anything in his way, easily frustrated and quick to throw a tantrum if he cannot get things to work*'. Gita is described by staff as '*delightful, a little star who is always keen to join in with the others and very articulate, always chattering*'.

> ### Critical Question
>
> How might staff in Case Study 8.1 record their concerns and what other professionals might they involve, if any?

Signposts to Theory

Tables 8.1 and 8.2 below illustrate the differences in how the theoretical approaches of Piaget, Freud, and Erikson explain this stage of development in the three children and how successful and unsuccessful progression might affect them later in life.

Table 8.1 Contrasting explanations

Stage	Key features
Preconceptual (Piaget)	Increasing engagement in imaginative and symbolic play with greater use of words and symbols to represent objects and people.
Anal (Freud)	Children are becoming aware that their own needs may conflict with others and are beginning to experience themselves as individuals.
Autonomy versus shame (Erikson)	Children are developing independence and autonomy and learning that they have choices.

Table 8.2 Progression through stages

Stage	Successful	Unsuccessful
Preconceptual (Piaget)	Play and language become more sophisticated.	Play and language remain immature.
Anal (Freud)	A greater sense of the need to respect the needs of others.	Overly stubborn and even miserly in adulthood with an exaggerated respect for authority.
Autonomy versus shame (Erikson)	Children feel confident and secure.	Over dependency on others in later life and feelings of self-doubt and low self-esteem.

Through social learning children acquire new understanding

Drawing upon Freud's *Psychodynamic* theory we can see that all three children are in the 'anal' stage of development. Robbie is not yet toilet trained, wears nappies to nursery each day and staff have noted that he presents as having significant issues with toileting. Pradeep and Gita on the other hand are confident in their use of the toilet. Applying the principles of Freud's theoretical approach, we can hypothesise that as an adult Robbie may demonstrate some aspects of his personality that are related to early issues around toileting and more particularly the extremely strict and at times aggressive responses of his parents. According to this approach, Robbie is repressing his feelings and emotions whilst Pradeep and Gita are internalising a stronger sense of security and stability.

Looking to the approach offered by Erikson we see that all three children are now at that stage when children are developing their sense of autonomy, but for Robbie, this is not the case. It is at this stage, Erikson suggested, that there lies the potential for inner conflicts between 'shame' and 'doubt'. Unlike Robbie, Pradeep and Gita are learning to be more independent and autonomous and, importantly, learning that they have choice; they are developing their self-confidence and self-efficacy, which will make them more confident and independent learners in the future. Robbie, in contrast, is internalising self-doubt and learning to be overly dependent on others, both of which are indicators of future low self-esteem and academic performance. The adults working with Robbie will need to be aware that on those occasions when he is quiet and withdrawn he may well be hiding difficult and distressing emotions that he does not yet fully understand, and that will be shaping how he sees the world in which he is growing up. This feature of Robbie's social learning has been well expressed by Mercer (2018), who emphasised how 'Anger, fear, and pleasure are all related to a child's thinking and beliefs about the world, especially the social world...' (p. 149). Sadly, it appears that Robbie is already displaying early signs of attachment disorder coupled with signs of low self-confidence and poor self-efficacy.

If we now apply the approach offered by Vygotsky, we can hypothesise that important 'cultural tools' such as nursery rhymes, stories and pictures that are typically available to children in their homes are for Robbie almost non-existent. Robbie's parents do not sit with him and read stories from books – indeed, there are only a few books in his home – nor do they spend time cuddled up to him telling stories and singing nursery rhymes. We saw in Part Two how Vygotsky placed great importance on the cultures within which children grow up and the social patterns of behaviour that are passed on to them from one generation to the next. Indeed, he saw children's development less as an individual process and more as the sum of those relationships that children have with those around them. Children, he believed, do not grow up in isolation but from birth are immersed in social and cultural processes that are dynamic and are shaped by the interconnected relationships that children have with those around them. Applying this to Robbie's early experiences we can see that those important elements of social learning are largely missing, thus impacting on his overall development; the importance of this for his future development has been well-expressed by Wertsch (1981), who emphasised how, 'In the process of development, children begin to use the same forms of behaviour in relation to themselves and others initially used in relation to them' (p. 164).

We also saw in Part Two how Vygotsky believed that children are born with an innate ability to learn through guidance from significant others who mediate their learning by providing a 'bridge' from their innate abilities to the internalisation of more advanced learning, 'Every function in the child's cultural development appears twice... first, between people (interpsychological), and then inside the child (intrapsychological)' (1978: 57). Applying this to Robbie, we can see that with the first of these, his cultural development is impoverished as his parents fail to act as a 'bridge' in mediating growth in his early learning to more advanced intellectual functioning. In contrast, Pradeep and Gita's parents have on a daily basis read them stories and talked about the pictures in their story books and about events in their environments, in sensitive and loving tones, and in this way have passed on those important cultural tools that Vygotsky saw as crucial to social development and learning.

> ### Chapter Link
> See Chapter 3 for details on Vygotsky's concept of social learning.

Insights into Robbie's Difficulties with Separation

We know from Part Two that as infants increasingly experience separation, they come to internalise representations of the absent primary caregiver and in doing so learn that their primary caregivers will return and they will not be harmed by these instances of separation, which are in fact temporary. In this way they become prepared for learning outside of the family, in new settings such as playgroups, nurseries, and primary school. This natural process is fundamental to secure attachment and facilitates later independence in learning and an increased ability to work collaboratively within, for example, problem-solving activities during what Piaget has called the *concrete operational* and *formal operational* stages. When secure attachment fails, however, as in the case of Robbie, then children experience disordered attachment, with the result that the quality of subsequent learning experiences can be significantly and adversely affected. Children such as Robbie may devote far too much of their emotional energy to anxious thoughts about their home situation and even feelings of loss and abandonment, all at the expense of their education and learning.

We can hypothesise, given the work of Ainsworth and the later work of Main and Solomon (1986) and Pearce (2009) that Robbie is presenting with characteristics of *insecurely attached/avoidance* and *insecurely attached/ambivalence* as suggested by his limited consistency in responses when reunited with his parents following separation – what Pearce (2009) referred to as '…contradictory behaviours… such as… approaching the caregiver only to stop and stare before full physical reunion occurs…' (p. 23). This appears evident from the comments made by staff at his nursery who noted that when Robbie is reunited with his parents he '*displays contradictory behaviour patterns such as wanting to be close to his parents but making little eye contact with them, approaching his parents but stopping and staring before making physical contact*'.

> ### Chapter Link
> Revisit Chapter 2 for details on Ainsworth's characteristics of attachment.

The *behaviourist* and *evolutionary* approaches to explaining attachment that were discussed in Chapter 2 can also help us understand and explain Robbie's emerging difficulties with separation and attachment and the impact of these on his emotional and social development and early learning.

Behaviourist Interpretation

Like any new-born infant Robbie needed milk to survive. His early positive attachment, therefore, should have been reinforced through developing associations between receiving milk and feeling the physical presence and comfort of being close to his mother, explained in Part Two by *classical conditioning*, but this did not happen; instead, Robbie was often left to cry for long periods of time when hungry and put away in another room so that his crying would not interfere with what his parents were doing. In this way, underlying associations were being formed between his emotional needs and the absence of physical presence and comfort from his parents. Equally, when Robbie smiled and made pleasing baby noises such as cooing these ought to have been responded to by his mother and father in a comforting way and thereby reinforced; this could be explained by what the *behaviourists* termed *operant conditioning*.

Evolutionary Interpretation

If we apply the *evolutionary* approach then we would accept that at birth Robbie was already programmed biologically to form attachments which were necessary for him to be nurtured and to feel safe and secure, but in Robbie's case this natural programming became distorted. When Robbie cried, for example, this behaviour should have evoked within his parents physical responses that were comforting, thereby offering him a sense of security. We know from reading the work of Schaffer and Emerson (1964) in Chapter 2 that Robbie would have been capable of developing multiple attachments, for example with his father if this was not happening naturally with his mother. In Robbie's case, neither parent afforded him the necessary means to form a positive attachment. It is important to emphasise that the *behaviourist* and *evolutionary* approaches are not mutually exclusive, but rather help us with understanding and explaining what is a complicated process.

Case Study 8.2: Giving Meaning to Assessments

Jamie has just turned seven and, as his birthday falls in July, he is nearly a whole year younger than many children in his class. He has just completed end-of-year formal testing in which he did not perform very well. The tests were conducted over one day and the results formally recorded. Following the summer holidays Jamie starts at a new school and the formal report written by his old school is passed to them; it reads '*Jamie is a pleasant and likeable child who tries hard but finds many aspects of learning to*

be challenging... he struggles with most areas of the curriculum... his reading and spelling are very weak'. Following his move to the new school Jamie's class teacher gives time to working individually with him as she believes that he is more capable than his previous school's report would suggest. She begins by teaching him new strategies for approaching maths, explaining problems in simple ways, breaking elements into smaller more manageable units and adapting more of a precision-based approach to his learning, giving him lots of praise when his attempts prove successful; she sees over the coming weeks that he begins to really enjoy maths, which is endorsed by his parents when she talks to them at the end of the school day. She also works at building his vocabulary and encouraging him to read widely, and ensures that he works with groups of able children who model good learning strategies and spoken language, and she observes each day how he increasingly imitates their actions and learning styles. She creates daily opportunities for Jamie to develop his self-confidence and self-efficacy by praising his efforts in front of other children and focusing his attention on those particular aspects of learning that he does well. Jamie begins to make new friends with some of the more able children in his class and he grows to love reading. His teacher observes how his self-confidence is growing, evidenced by his willingness to approach new tasks that require him to problem-solve, and to offer suggestions when he is working as part of a group.

Critical Question

Why do teachers assess children in different ways, and how might elements of Feuerstein's theoretical approach improve practice with assessment?

Signposts to Theory

In Jamie's old school he was asked to undertake a 'static' assessment, which involved him being formally tested on one specific day with tests designed to measure attainments in English and mathematics as opposed to assessing his potential and underlying competencies and what he might be capable of when given the correct type of support. We saw from Frederickson and Cline (2002) in Chapter 5 that such tests largely ignore levels of maturity; in Jamie's case he was nearly a year younger than many children in his class, and his intellectual development – as Piagetian theory would suggest – had probably not matured to a level commensurate with those of his older classmates. Jamie's new teacher is aware of this and engages more directly with assessing his potential to learn and what Vygotsky referred to as the *zone of proximal development* as opposed to limiting her assessment of his abilities to his attainments in English and mathematics, or his *zone of actual development*.

When Jamie moved schools, his new teacher felt intuitively that he was more capable than had been reported by his previous school, because she made time to observe his behaviours, especially the strategies he employed when asked to approach problem-solving activities, and engaged in dialogue with him about why he used these strategies. She focused on teaching him new strategies for learning spellings and for approaching mathematical activities, which is in keeping with the emphasis Vygotsky and Bruner placed on adults supporting children with new learning, discussed in Part Two. She also provided daily opportunities for Jamie to demonstrate his successes with new learning in front of his peers, and in this way she set about reinforcing his self-concept, which is in keeping with the principles of *behaviourist* theory and more particularly *operant conditioning* that was discussed in Chapter 3. His new teacher also reinforced his use of newly learned strategies by again offering praise, especially when he initiated these himself; in this way, she was again employing the principles of *operant conditioning*. Over time, she assessed Jamie's potential to learn when given new strategies and opportunities to develop his self-confidence and, in this way, she was employing a 'dynamic' approach to assessment, in contrast to the 'static' approach employed in his previous school, which is in keeping with the ideas of Feuerstein discussed in Chapter 5. Her approach enabled her, therefore, to gain deeper and more accurate insights into Jamie's potential and underlying abilities, and importantly his capacity to 'learn how to learn'.

Chapter Link

Revisit Chapter 5 for details on Feuerstein's ideas on learning how to learn.

Informed observation of learning tells us so much about intellectual functioning

The philosophy of learning that underpinned teaching and assessment in Jamie's new school was based largely on the theoretical approaches offered by Vygotsky and Bruner, and more recently Feuerstein, all of whom emphasised the importance of dialogue and adults mediating learning through language, for example by listening carefully, asking focused and relevant questions and importantly seeing questioning as a valuable means of extending language and therefore thinking. The importance of dialogue for children's education was also addressed by others, for example by Freire in Part Two.

> ## Chapter Link
> Revisit Chapter 4 for details on Freire's thoughts on the importance of dialogue.

Jamie's new teacher was in effect structuring his learning in small steps and employing 'scaffolding' where learning proved challenging for him, which is in line with Bruner's theoretical approach. She was also supporting him in becoming a more independent learner by actively shaping the teaching environment to progress his thinking and learning through encouraging him to apply reasoning and logic in problem-solving activities. She understood the immense importance of 'imitation' in early childhood learning and how this process could be enhanced by having Jamie work alongside his peers, a key element in Bandura's theory of *Social Learning*.

It is also useful to draw upon *Attribution Theory* to help us understand Jamie's learning. This theory has its roots in the work of Heider (1958), who suggested that individuals typically act as 'naïve' psychologists in their attempts to make sense of their worlds by constructing relationships between 'cause' and 'effect', even when there are none. Heider focused on internal (dispositional) causes and external (situational) causes that he believed individuals employ when attributing meaning to events. More recently, Fiske and Taylor (1991), cited by McLeod (2012), suggested that this theory '…deals with how the social perceiver uses information to arrive at causal explanations for events' (p. 23). A frequently cited explanation of *Attribution Theory* is that offered by Kelley (1967), cited in McLeod (2012), known as the *Covariation Model*, which differentiates between actions judged or attributed to particular characteristics of an individual (dispositional) and to those of the environment (situational). McLeod has explained 'covariation' as being when individuals have access to information:

> …from multiple observations, at different times and situations, and can perceive the covariation of an observed effect and its causes… In trying to discover the causes of behavior people act like scientists.

McLeod goes on to suggest that when making judgements, i.e. attributions, individuals draw upon three types of evidence:

Consensus: the extent to which other people behave in the same way in a similar situation... **Distinctiveness**: the extent to which the person behaves in the same way in similar situations... **Consistency**: the extent to which the person behaves like this every time the situation occurs.

We can see that in Jamie's case teachers at his former school placed greater emphasis on dispositional factors, attributing Jamie's slower progress largely to internal dispositional factors such as his perceived limited ability, whilst the teacher at his new school placed greater emphasis on situational factors, believing that by changing the environment in which Jamie learned she could then alter and develop his dispositional factors.

We can also draw on the ideas of Nel Noddings discussed in Chapter 2, who drew a distinction between teachers who care in the 'virtue' sense and those who care in the 'relational' sense. We might assume that Jamie's teacher in his old school cared in the 'virtue' sense in that she was conscientious, followed aims and objectives and worked hard to inspire her pupils to achieve goals and succeed academically, but may have been 'unable to establish relations of care and trust' in the 'relational sense' with Jamie, unlike the teacher in his new school who employed greater levels of empathy and was determined to explore Jamie's unique and individual needs. In addition, Jamie's new teacher may have thought beyond the challenges imposed by external factors such as her school's perceived need to follow a set curriculum, her own perceived need to demonstrate that she had met externally imposed targets, and reported data gained through 'static' testing that has been imposed by policy and decision-makers over recent years.

Chapter Link

Revisit Chapter 3 for details on Noddings' ideas on teaching in the 'virtue' sense.

Discussion Point

Should teachers in Key Stage 1 be trained to make assessments of children who might be dyslexic?

Extended Reading

Hope, S. (2018) 'Principled professionalism in the classroom', in I. Luke and J. Gourd (eds), *Thriving as a Professional Teacher*. London: Routledge. This is an excellent chapter that explores the challenges faced by many teachers in the UK who are tasked with delivering an externally imposed curriculum.

Ofsted (2013) *What About the Children? Joint Working between Adult and Children's Services When Parents or Carers Have Mental Ill Health and/or Drug and Alcohol Problems*. Manchester: Office for Standards in Education. A comprehensive look into childhood today and the impact of societal issues on learning and development in childhood.

Roffey, S., Jamison, L. and Davis, C. (2016) 'Behaviour', in D. Wyse and S. Rogers (eds), *A Guide to Early Years & Primary Teaching*. London: Sage. This is an excellent chapter that looks at many social issues relating to behaviour; case studies also illustrate the points being made by the authors.

9

LANGUAGE AND LEARNING

Children who have good language skills at the age of five are much more likely to achieve well and to develop good social skills… It is impossible to overestimate the importance of helping children to develop their language and communication skills.

(Allott and Waugh, 2019: 264)

By the end of this chapter you should:

- understand the importance of language for learning in early childhood
- appreciate how different theoretical perspectives can help us understand and explain the complex nature of language development
- appreciate the challenges faced by children on the autistic spectrum and their families

Communication is at the heart of all social learning

Case Study 9.1: Robbie, Pradeep, and Gita Start School

Robbie, Pradeep and Gita have now all reached their fifth birthdays and have started at their local primary school. Robbie has been slow to develop his language and his teacher is already documenting concerns about his expressive language, which she describes as *'still very immature'*. She is especially concerned by his poor vocabulary and verbal comprehension, and his reluctance to initiate verbal interactions with other children, seemingly preferring to shout at them and on occasions smack them when he gets frustrated. He is also reluctant to play with other children and, where possible, avoids collaborating in group activities; a recent referral to the school's Educational Psychologist resulted in a further referral to the Speech and Language Therapy Service. Pradeep, on the other hand, enjoys playing with his peers, likes to initiate interactions and has already acquired a wide vocabulary. Pradeep, however, struggles at times with physical activities and is very clumsy, often falling over and bumping into things and he still cannot ride his two-wheeled bicycle without stabilisers on the wheels. He also has problems with getting himself dressed, using utensils when eating, climbing stairs, balancing, and playing games – especially those that involve throwing and catching a ball. In contrast, Gita continues to be very outgoing and creative though her parents often comment that she *'is hopelessly forgetful'* and *'seems to have word-finding difficulties and problems with recognising letters and making the sounds of letters'*, which the reception teacher assures them is *'nothing to worry about'.*

Discussion Point

Should teachers in Key Stage 1 be expected to identify language problems?

Signposts to Theory

All three children are now at the stage when language needs to be more sophisticated and progression with reading and writing is being carefully monitored. In terms of their development they are, according to Piaget's framework, in the *intuitive* stage (4 to 7 years), the second sub-stage of the *preoperational* stage (2 to 7 years) when cognitive development allows children to decentre and when vocabulary and verbal comprehension should be more advanced. According to Freud's stages, they are entering the *latency* stage (5/6 years through to puberty) when sexual energy is increasingly directed towards activities such as friendships, which is important for language development; children at this stage are increasingly developing their language through play and through the relationships they form with other children, as well as with their teachers and other significant adults. Drawing on Erikson's theory, we see that the children are moving from the *initiative versus guilt* stage (3 to 5 years), when they are acquiring an ability to empathise, to the *industry versus inferiority* stage, when winning the approval of peers becomes very important.

Common to each of these theoretical approaches is the strong emphasis they place on language development. Table 9.1 below summarises the different explanations offered by key theorists regarding language development in childhood that were discussed in previous chapters.

Table 9.1 Contrasting explanations

Approach	Key features
Behaviourists	Children learn by imitating those around them.
Chomsky	Children create language themselves. The acquisition of language follows patterns such as acquiring the rules of grammar through what Chomsky termed the 'Language Acquisition Device'.
Vygotsky	By talking and listening to others, children develop and extend their own understanding and, in doing so, contribute to their communities and wider societies in which they live.

When we consider language in childhood it is likely that we think initially about spoken language. We may, for example, reflect on the acquisition of vocabulary and the use of phrases and sentences, which allow young children to increasingly externalise their thinking by communicating their thoughts and ideas to others; we may also reflect on the clarity of speech and vocal expression. There are, however, some children who experience difficulties with spoken or *expressive* language, for example, poor articulation and word-finding difficulties, and there are others who experience difficulties with *receptive* language where they may, for example, fail to understand what is being said to them, which can of course impact hugely on their learning, in addition to their social and emotional development. There will also be some children who experience difficulties with both *expressive* and *receptive* language, and for these children verbal communication can be extremely challenging. Non-verbal communication can also present significant challenges for these children, as well as those children on the autistic spectrum as will be seen in Case Study 9.2.

The importance of adults focusing on language development in childhood has been stressed by Head (2016: 37) who, for example, drew attention to how the Regio Emilia approach, discussed in Chapter 5, 'is based on a pedagogy of listening to the child's voice'; this approach also, as Head notes, recognises that 'children can express themselves in many different ways, with the task of the teacher being 'to seek and to hear the voice of the child…'. Teachers in Reggio Emilia employ questioning as a technique for improving children's comprehension and being directly involved in their children's learning, which should follow on from the experiences they have had in the home. The importance of these early language interactions in the home between child and parents and their relevance to Robbie, Pradeep and Gita's early learning can be seen in the following comments by Head, who has drawn attention to the much-cited work of Wells (1990) and the 'Bristol Language Development Project 1984', whose research focused on children's language in early childhood:

> Wells noted that children who made the most progress in terms of vocabulary learning were those who interacted with adults, who 'pick up and extend the meaning expressed in the child's previous utterance' (Wells, 1990: 3). This process requires adults to show genuine interest in children's ideas and conversation… (Head, 2016: 373)

Critical Question

What can Early Years practitioners and teachers in primary schools do to improve children's vocabulary and their verbal comprehension?

If we turn to Vygotsky's *social constructivist* approach to help us understand language development in all three children then we need to understand the emphasis that he places on social learning, which he proposed exists first at the 'intermental' level in the form of spoken language, and then at the 'intramental' level in the form of internal language, which we view as 'thinking' (Whitebread, 2012: 127). Here, it is worth reflecting on the language experiences of the three children and how these contrasted with one another. Whilst all three developed spoken language at the 'intermental' level, their experiences at the 'intramental' level would have been vastly different. Pradeep and Gita, for example, would have been afforded many opportunities to engage in conversation with their parents who would have conversed with them using quite sophisticated language, and in this way they would have enjoyed good modelling of language structures from their parents. In contrast, Robbie would typically have been ignored or shouted at.

> ## Chapter Link
> Revisit Chapter 3 for details on Vygotsky's social constructivist approach.

Gray and MacBlain (2015: 97) have offered a very useful illustration of Vygotsky's approach to developing language and thought, which can help in our understanding of the children's language development and learning, in which they note Vygotsky's four stages, *primitive, practical intelligence, external symbolic*, and *internalisation of symbolic tools*, beginning with the pre-verbal stage through to that stage when children internalise speech as thinking. It is now worth applying these stages to the development of each of the three children.

With the first, *primitive*, very young children, as Gray and MacBlain note, '…use vocal activity as a means of emotional expression and for social engagement', which would certainly have been the case for Pradeep and Gita but not for Robbie, whose vocal activity would have resulted in a very different type of emotional expression from his parents. Social engagement would have most likely been confined to being shouted at or put into a separate room for lengthy periods so his crying could not be heard; when, as an infant, he made 'cooing' and pleasing baby noises these would also, more often than not, have been ignored. Later, during the *external symbolic* stage when, as Gray and MacBlain indicate, 'thinking aloud is common' and language is 'used to help with internal problem solving' and to help children 'self-regulate and plan their activities' (2015: 97), we can hypothesise that whilst Pradeep and Gita were encouraged by their parents to think aloud when engaging in problem-solving activities, it is likely that Robbie's parents would have told him to keep quiet, which would undoubtedly have led to problems with self-regulating and planning his own play.

The final stage identified by Gray and MacBlain, *internalisation of symbolic tools*, is when children have increased their ability to think more independently and more flexibly. Again, we can see that by drawing on Vygotsky's approach all three children's experiences during this later stage of development would have been quite different. Pradeep and Gita would have developed greater flexibility in their thinking and greater independence when communicating their ideas, whilst Robbie in all probability would have suppressed many aspects of his thinking, which would have impacted negatively on how he communicated with others and formed relationships. We should also note here the importance that Vygotsky placed on 'cultural' tools such as stories, nursery rhymes and art, which in Robbie's case were scarce, again most certainly impacting negatively on his early language development.

We can also turn to Erikson's theoretical model discussed in Chapter 2 and look at his *initiative versus guilt* stage (3 to 5 years), when children's language is improving and they are developing the ability to empathise with others. Excessive control at this stage, as was the case with Robbie, may result in subsequent feelings of guilt that present later in adolescence and adulthood as a lack of initiative and that can impact negatively on learning. Erikson also drew attention to how during this stage children typically engage in asking lots of questions, emphasising that if children's requests for answers went unheeded and were not given appropriate status then, again, feelings of guilt accompanied by embarrassment and shame might follow later and lessen the degree to which children would seek to interact and communicate with others. We can hypothesise that it is likely that this will be Robbie's experience later in life.

The impact of Robbie, Pradeep and Gita's language development in the home can be further understood if we draw on the ideas offered by Bruner in Chapter 4. Like Vygotsky, Bruner placed a great deal of emphasis on the important role that culture plays in children's language development and how culture shapes and even defines how some parents think and communicate; this has been well explained by Smidt (2011: 66):

> Bruner reminds us that 'Children learn to use language initially… to get what they want, to play games, to stay connected with those on whom they are dependent. In doing so, they find the constraints that prevail in the culture around them embodied in their parents' restrictions and conventions' (Bruner, 1983, p. 103).

We can assume that in the case of Robbie, his parents' responses to his first cries, words and phrases rarely met any of his emotional needs and probably failed to help him stay 'connected' to his parents on whom he was 'dependent'. We can hypothesise that *'the constraints that prevail in the culture'* around Robbie and which were *'embodied'* in his parents' *'restrictions and conventions'* would have reduced his opportunities to communicate positively and in a rewarding way with others who might have broadened and stimulated his intellectual and cognitive development.

Drawing again on the work of Bruner and the idea of *scaffolding* we know that Bruner saw cognitive and language development in young children being influenced by how adults and more particularly parents share experiences with them. Citing Bruner (1975, 1983), Jones (2016) has explained this process most eloquently, as follows:

> This 'parent-child interaction' is the context within which adults help children with their learning and language development. They do this by *scaffolding* learning: by showing children how to learn new skills based on what the children already know, while using language that is adapted to support the children's understanding (Bruner, 1983). (Jones, 2016: 27)

When we apply Bruner's notion of 'parent-child interaction' as noted by Jones, we can hypothesise that Pradeep and Gita would have experienced positive interactions with their parents who invested time in articulating and sharing experiences and the meaning of these experiences with them; in effect, their parents would have *scaffolded* new learning. They would have done this, for example, by taking time to introduce them to new vocabulary and new concepts and, very importantly, to listen to them. In contrast, the 'parent-child interaction' experienced by Robbie with his parents would have been limited and the process of *scaffolding* that was so valuable for Pradeep and Gita would for Robbie have been almost non-existent; little time was given by his parents to introducing new vocabulary and new concepts and articulating new experiences, with much of his learning at home happening largely on a random basis.

Discussion Point

How might Early Years practitioners advise parents who show little interest in developing their children's language?

Sharing experiences offers adults a wonderful means of observing learning in young children

Case Study 9.2: Asperger's Syndrome

Craig is 7 years of age and, following discussion with his parents, the school's Special Educational Needs and Disability Coordinator (SENDCo) makes a referral to the Educational Psychologist in which she emphasises how '*Craig has always had difficulty in making friends and struggles with change; he is more of a loner and this is especially noticeable during break times outside of the classroom where he does not really play with others and rarely gets involved in games*'. The Educational Psychologist assesses Craig and reports that he is of above average intellectual ability but with significant communication difficulties; she also refers Craig to a paediatrician who confirms that Craig is on the autistic spectrum and reports a diagnosis of Asperger's Syndrome.

Critical Question

What other professionals might Early Years practitioners and teachers in primary schools work with to support children with Asperger's Syndrome?

Craig's behaviours are typical of many children with the condition known as Asperger's Syndrome (AS) and who are on the autistic spectrum. It is now accepted that 'Asperger's Syndrome is due to a dysfunction of specific structures and systems in the brain. In short, the brain is "wired" differently, not necessarily defective…' (Attwood, 2007: 327). Mayes and Calhoun (2003: 15) have commented as follows:

> Many experts now agree that autism is a spectrum disorder and that Asperger syndrome (AS) is high-functioning or mild autism… However, controversy persists, and 'Asperger syndrome' remains a popular term used by clinicians and parents alike.

Having a better understanding of the needs of children with Asperger's Syndrome has in recent decades improved perceptions of how children like Craig can be best supported as they make transitions from home to Early Years settings and then primary school, and subsequently to post-primary education. A great deal of our understanding of the needs of these children has emerged from research studies that have sought to understand and explain how the brain functions. Attwood (2007: 327) has, for example, described how research studies have confirmed how this syndrome:

> …is associated with a dysfunction of the 'social brain', which comprises components of the frontal and temporal regions of the cortex… There is also evidence of dysfunction of the amygdala, the basal ganglia and cerebellum… The latest research suggests that there is weak connectivity between these components… There is also evidence

to suggest right hemisphere cortical dysfunction… and an abnormality of the dopamine system… Thus, we now know which structures in the brain are functioning or 'wired' differently.

Attwood has proposed that for most individuals with Asperger's Syndrome the differences in brain development are due to genetic factors (2007: 328). Drawing upon the earlier work of Attwood (1993), Herbert (2005) offers a useful range of interventions that teachers, such as in the case of Craig's teacher, might use for children with this condition:

- provision, as far as possible, of a predictable environment and consistent routines… allowing opportunities for social interaction and facilitation of social relationships in fairly structured and supervised activities;
- preparation for alterations in routines or timetabling;
- issuing of brief, precise, and specific instructions…;
- reducing tasks into manageable segments…;
- not expecting the student to have the ability unaided, to generalise instructions… (pp. 187–8)

Craig's teacher needs to create a classroom environment with clear boundaries and rules for all children. It is essential that Craig is provided with support for acquiring strategies that he can use within the classroom to support new learning, an example of which would be using a visual timetable so that he can see at a glance what he needs to do at any one time, and importantly where and when change is due to take place. A most useful insight offered some years ago by one individual diagnosed with this condition has been provided by Wendy Lawson (2013: 190), who offered the following regarding her own early years:

> If people only see the negative and constantly tell you what you are doing wrong, then your self-esteem plunges… I was fortunate to encounter a couple of people who decided to give me some of their time… I tended to be left to my own devices often. This isn't ideal for children with autism. We benefit more from early intervention and activities that keep us 'connected' to life. (2013: 188–9)

Having a diagnosis can help both young people and adults with Asperger's Syndrome to understand themselves and to know that they are not, for example, unintelligent and that whilst they have limitations these are not just confined to them. One further important insight offered by Lawson is of her social and verbal interactions with others:

> Someone might just be speaking to me. However, I experience it as someone projecting into my thinking or conversation, and I feel almost violated! 'How dare they interrupt my space and distract me from my course. Didn't they understand that now I would have to start over again, recapping my thoughts or plans, and schedule it all again… understanding everyday life requires an understanding of

'concepts' – concepts such as right, wrong, time, space... Most of the time I got into trouble at school because I didn't have a concept for what was being said, done, or expected. (2013: 192)

We can see from Craig's learning that his social development and particularly his communication with others impacts on many aspects of his learning.

We can draw on the work of Bronfenbrenner to help us contextualise the complexities in the wider communities and societies that children like Craig and his family need to negotiate throughout early as well as later childhood. In contrast to Bandura's *Social Learning* theory, Bronfenbrenner's *Ecological Model of Individual Development* emphasises how children's own biologies play a central role in learning, and the interrelationship between children and their environments, through his idea of layers.

> ## Chapter Link
>
> Revisit Chapter 3, Figure 3.2 for Bronfenbrenner's *Ecological Model*.

Bronfenbrenner believed that every child is born with a unique biology and even from birth interrelates differently with their environments and others around them, and later with the different communities of which they will be a part. As a young child Craig will have had to make transitions from the security and familiarity of his home into pre-school and then primary school, and relate to different children and adults in addition to managing frequent and often unpredictable change, which will have been very challenging for him. Change, however, cannot be avoided; take, for example, the fact that as this book is being written, Early Years settings and schools have had to close because of the COVID-19 pandemic, and children like Craig are having to deal with the stark and unpredictable changes that this has brought about in their lives, which is extremely challenging. In addition to this, we can use Bronfenbrenner's model again to see how other wider economic and political influences and decisions made nationally and across the globe impact on schools throughout the UK due to COVID-19.

We can also draw on the ideas of Rogoff (2003) discussed in Chapter 3 to help us understand and explain Craig's situation. Like Bronfenbrenner, and indeed Vygotsky and Bruner, Rogoff emphasised how development does not just happen within children themselves but within dynamic group and community processes of which children are an integral part. Like Bandura and Bruner, she emphasises the importance of social context and environment on learning and stresses how children learn alongside others. If we want to understand learning and development, she argues, then we need to understand children's learning not just in their family life but also in their communities where, for example, many children benefit from being taken by their parents to playgroups, pre-school activity centres and local parent-child groups which will be advantageous for their language development. This perspective is most helpful because it causes us to focus not only on the shifting and complex dynamics within Craig's family and within Craig himself, but also importantly on those wider processes in the different communities of which he is an integral part.

Discussion Point

If Early Years practitioners or Key Stage 1 teachers suspect that a child is on the autistic spectrum, who should they discuss their concerns with, and at what point should they involve the parents?

Extended Reading

Allott, K. and Waugh, D. (2019) 'Talk and communication: couldn't they just sit down and shut up', in C. Carden (ed.), *Primary Teaching*. London: Sage. This is an accessible and very readable chapter, which offers insights into language in the primary classroom together with practical strategies for teachers.

National Educational Psychological Service (NEPS) (2015) *Children with Language Difficulties in Primary School: Teacher Guidelines & Strategies for In-Class Support*. Available at: www.education.ie/en/Schools-Colleges/Services/National-Educational-Psychological-Service-NEPS-/NEPS-Guides/Language-Skills/Language-Difficulties-Guidance-for-Teachers-and-Strategies-for-In-Class-Support-Primary.pdf (accessed: 3 October 2020). This is a document prepared by the educational psychological service of Ireland which explains the nature of expressive and receptive language difficulties in children, as well as offering excellent strategies for teachers.

Jones, M. (2016) *Talking and Learning with Young Children*. London: Sage. This is an excellent text; accessible and comprehensive, and full of useful case studies and ideas for Early Years practitioners and teachers.

10

HEALTH AND WELLBEING

By the end of this chapter you should:

- understand the importance of accurate early assessment in childhood and how difficulties that go unnoticed in the first years can impact detrimentally on children's later learning
- appreciate the importance of Early Years practitioners and teachers in primary schools working multi-professionally to support the emotional development of children from dysfunctional homes
- understand the importance of good health and wellbeing in childhood and its impact on early learning
- appreciate the need for children to have a balanced diet and the part this plays in ensuring good health and wellbeing in children
- appreciate how healthy eating is important in helping children's brains achieve their functional potential and that overeating the wrong type of food can lead to obesity and impact on social and emotional learning

Case Study 10.1: Robbie, Pradeep, and Gita Prepare for Key Stage 2

All three children are now nearing the end of Key Stage 1. Robbie is meeting weekly with a member of the school's Behaviour Support Service and his social worker remains concerned about his general health, poor physical development, and emotional wellbeing. Pradeep is causing concerns because of his lack of general progress and immaturity; his GP has referred him to a pediatrician because of his extreme clumsiness and poor organisation and his parents' concerns about his illegible handwriting. After meeting with the pediatrician Pradeep is diagnosed as having dyspraxia. Gita continues to be viewed as an affable child but has been struggling with reading, though her teachers praise her for her creativity; she is now developing strategies for avoiding reading. Gita's parents have spoken with her teacher who has assured them that she is *'probably a late developer'* and that *'given time she will learn to read but we don't want to push her too much at this stage'.* Her parents, however, have now requested an independent assessment by an Educational Psychologist who, after assessing Gita, reports as follows:

Extract from Educational Psychologist's report

I recently assessed Gita's intellectual functioning and literacy and, on this occasion, she achieved the centile scores indicated in Table 10.1.

Table 10.1 Results of assessment

Intellectual functioning		Literacy	
Index	**Centile**	**Test**	**Centile**
Perceptual Reasoning	92	Word recognition	3
Verbal Comprehension	85	Reading Comprehension	15
Working Memory	1	Spelling	4
Processing Speed	5		

Two-thirds of children are considered to function within the average range of ability as represented by the 16th and 84th centiles. The 99th centile represents the top one per cent of ability and the 1st centile represents the lowest one per cent of ability.

The above results suggest that Gita has specific learning difficulties that are severe and that are typically found amongst children with dyslexia. Gita's centile scores on Working Memory and Processing Speed Indexes are well below the average range and in contrast to those on the Perceptual Reasoning and Verbal Comprehension Indexes, which clearly indicate that she is intellectually very able and above average intelligence. Gita clearly experiences significant difficulties with individual word recognition and decoding and is confused by the whole process of 'spelling'. Her confusion combined with her overuse of inefficient strategies underpinned by very weak working memory results in Gita finding the whole process of 'spelling' extremely challenging. Gita will, therefore, need to acquire different strategies for tackling spelling, word recognition and decoding. She will also need appropriate interventions for increasing her motivation to read and comprehend what she is reading. It will be important that Gita's true potential is properly recognised. Given Gita's specific weaknesses with Working Memory and Processing Speed I recommend that greater emphasis is placed on developing a multisensory approach, which involves kinaesthetic memory. I also offer the following recommendations:

- Literacy teaching should be structured, cumulative, sequential, and multi-sensory.
- Lots of opportunities to engage in over-learning of new material.
- Acquiring strategies to improve working memory and processing speed.
- Developing a better understanding of basic spelling principles.
- Increasing Gita's knowledge of sound/symbol correspondence and syllabification.
- Gita should develop cursive writing linked to her multi-sensory learning.

Critical Question

When might Early Years practitioners and teachers in primary schools need to involve an Educational Psychologist?

Signposts to Theory

All three children are now in the second sub-stage of the *preoperational* stage (2 to 7 years), the *intuitive* (4 to 7 years) when, according to Piaget, children are developing their cognitive skills and abilities to a level that will allow them to remove themselves from situations and think more abstractly. Their language abilities should be relatively well advanced, and they should be capable of seeing others' points of view more readily. If we turn to Freud's original stages we see that the three children are in the *latency* stage (5/6 years through to puberty) when sexual energy is directed towards activities such as hobbies and friendships, with play becoming more evident with other children of the same gender. According to Erikson's theory the children are in the *industry versus inferiority* stage, where their teachers have become important role models and winning the approval of others and especially their peers is very important as this gives them a greater sense of pride in their achievements and who they are. Successful progression through the stages identified by Piaget, Freud and Erikson leads to growth in emotional, social, and cognitive functioning whilst unsuccessful progression can result in difficulties in adolescence and adulthood (see Tables 10.2 and 10.3).

Table 10.2 Contrasting explanations

Stage	Key features
Intuitive	Cognitive skills and abilities allow children to decentre and see others' points of view.
Latency	A period of exploration when sexual energy, though remaining present in the child, is nevertheless repressed and is sublimated into areas external to the child such as sports and friendships.
Industry versus inferiority	Teachers are important role models and winning approval from peers is particularly important, as is taking pride in achievements.

Table 10.3 Progression through stages

Stage	Successful	Unsuccessful
Intuitive	Children learn to empathise with others.	Children's emotional intelligence remains immature.
Latency	Good social and communication skills and self-confidence.	Immaturity and difficulties with forming fulfilling relationships in adulthood.
Industry versus inferiority	Confidence in the ability to succeed and to be industrious.	Feelings of inferiority and self-doubt and lacking in a sense of competence.

Robbie

In Chapter 2 we looked at the work of Salovey and Mayer (1990) who saw four key factors as central to developing good emotional intelligence: *perceiving, reasoning, understanding,* and *managing* emotions. If we reflect on the experiences Robbie has had in his family life, we can hypothesise that all of these were, to a significant degree, absent in his life. In *perceiving* his parents' emotional responses to his own behaviours as well as to each other he would have found a stark contrast between these and the emotional responses of adults at his nursery and primary school, which would have been far more measured and empathetic as opposed to being mostly aggressive and lacking in consistency.

Piagetian theory would suggest that Robbie may not have reached a level of cognitive development by which he can effectively apply reason to *understanding* the emotional responses of others as well as his own feelings; we can infer, therefore, that this would have caused him great confusion; his underdeveloped intellectual capacity for reasoning would have been negatively affected by his home background. Pradeep and Gita's parents, in contrast, would have taken time to explain with sensitivity why particular behaviours were unacceptable and what Pradeep and Gita might do to change these. Robbie was in fact not being supported at home with *understanding* and *managing* his emotions, which Salovey and Mayer viewed as critical to developing good emotional intelligence.

If we draw on Goleman's contribution to our understanding of emotional intelligence discussed in Chapter 2, which viewed children as falling into three distinctive styles for dealing with emotions, *self-aware*, *engulfed* and *accepting*, we can hypothesise that Robbie's self-awareness in regard to his feelings and emotions was limited, as these were rarely – if ever – explored in any real depth by his parents. Robbie's early experiences were in stark contrast to those of Pradeep and Gita whose parents took the time to develop their self-awareness of feelings by supporting them in managing emotions that they experienced but did not as yet have the cognitive capacity to properly understand. We can suggest, therefore, that Robbie would have found himself frequently *engulfed* by feelings and emotions that he did not understand and that often swamped his thinking when at school and when he was supposed to be engaged in learning tasks and activities.

Discussion Point

Is it helpful to think of emotional development in terms of stages, and how useful are terms such as '*oral*', '*anal*', '*latency*' and '*industry versus inferiority*' to adults working with young children?

If we look at the ideas offered by Rogoff discussed in Chapter 3 we see that, like Vygotsky, she emphasised how children develop as participants in their cultural communities and that development doesn't just occur within children themselves but within those *dynamic* group and *community* processes of which children are an integral part. In Robbie's case such *dynamic* and *community* processes were limited by his parents' lifestyle and restricted to his parents' friends who also lived dysfunctional lives; he therefore had limited access to what Rogoff referred to as 'outsiders', as in the case of groups outside of his home such as social clubs, church groups and sports clubs. Robbie's teachers would need to understand that whilst he could form his own ideas as an 'insider' in his family, to use Rogoff's term, these were rarely if ever talked about and explored by his parents, and therefore never properly developed. Robbie also lacked those important opportunities, emphasised by Rogoff, to learn alongside positive adult role models and participate in his cultural community and community processes. Since birth, Robbie has also had a poor diet, which has impacted on his energy levels. Poor quality of sleep has also been an issue for Robbie because there is insufficient heating in the house and he frequently goes to bed feeling very cold at night; an almost total lack of routine at home has also added to his insecurity.

Robbie's educational future looks bleak. Some years ago, the Children and Young People's Mental Health Coalition (CYPMHC, 2012) published a guide for headteachers aimed at preventing emotional and behavioural difficulties in children. The guide highlighted how pupils with conduct disorder, as in the case of Robbie, are more likely to experience problems with the acquisition of literacy and numeracy skills, leading to poor self-efficacy and internalised perceptions of themselves as failures. The CYPMHC distinguished between *conduct disorder*, defined as 'a repetitive and persistent behaviour problem, where major age-appropriate societal norms or the basic rights of others are violated', and *emotional disorder*, which refers to 'conditions such as depression and anxiety' (p. 4). We can hypothesise that it is likely that Robbie may at some stage be assessed as having *conduct* and *emotional* disorders. The guide also offered what is a disturbing reflection that casts light on how Robbie's condition is not isolated to him: '…1 in 10 or at least 3 young people in every class has a behavioural or emotional difficulty' (p. 4).

Gita

The profile of difficulties offered in the case of Gita is typical of many children in early childhood with dyslexia. It must be said that dyslexia remains a contentious area, with some still denying that there is such a condition, whilst others continue to debate the usefulness of the label 'dyslexia' and what in essence the term actually means (Everatt and Reid, 2009; MacBlain et al., 2017). Gita's emerging difficulties with literacy as she moves towards Key Stage 2 clearly emphasise the importance of early identification which, if this fails to happen, leads to children internalising feelings of failure that then impact on their self-esteem and self-efficacy as discussed in Chapter 2. Crombie and Reid (2009) have stressed that '… if early identification is to be effective then it is important that it focuses on pre-school children as well as children in the early years of primary school' (p. 71). Indeed, they go on to assert how:

> It is often the case, in a local authority context, that a child has to *fail* to learn to read and write before difficulties are recognised, and certainly before the term 'dyslexia' can be used. This means there is a delay in providing effective provision… (pp. 71–2)

Early literacy skills offer children new ways of communicating

We can see that Gita has been failing even in her pre-school years with the basics of reading and writing. Whilst her parents felt intuitively since she first began school that something was preventing Gita from making progress in reading, they were unable to persuade the school to action appropriate assessment from a literacy specialist or the school's Special Educational Needs Coordinator (SENCO). They decided, therefore, to pay for an independent assessment by an Educational Psychologist, which then revealed the actual underlying specific learning difficulties that were preventing Gita from making good progress with her reading and writing. Had an assessment been carried out when Gita was younger this would have avoided a great deal of anxiety and frustration on the part of Gita and her parents. When planning to meet the learning needs of children like Gita who have dyslexia, Reid and Came (2009: 198–9) have emphasised that it is the responsibility of the school and not just individual teachers. They have also stressed the need for 'accurate and full assessment' of each child's attainments as being central to any planning, and for the accurate assessment of listening comprehension, in addition to reading accuracy and reading fluency, for as Reid (2009) has pointed out '…it is often the discrepancy between listening or reading comprehension and reading accuracy that can be a key factor in identifying dyslexia' (p. 199).

Critical Question

What sort of information should Early Years practitioners and teachers in primary schools collect before making a referral to an Educational Psychologist of a child who is presenting with significant learning difficulties?

It is also helpful here to draw upon the ideas discussed in Chapter 5 regarding the contribution that is being made by *neuroscience*. The benefits of drawing upon neuroscience to help us understand Gita's specific learning difficulties in the areas of *working memory* and *processing speed* can be seen in the following from Drysdale (2009), who commented on how:

> To become a skilled reader, the young learner must create entirely new neurological circuitry connecting visual, auditory and motor systems at lightning speed. Development of the skills within any one of these systems and the learner's ability to make neural connections at speed will affect success in learning to read. (p. 237)

We can see in the recommendations made by the Educational Psychologist who assessed Gita that she places great emphasis on multisensory learning, which is key to learning for children with dyslexia, as was stressed recently by MacBlain et al. (2015):

> Teaching should be: Structured… Sequential… Cumulative… Multisensory – this is, perhaps, the most important element of all and involves the development of kinaesthetic memory… Children should not experience failure. This is where the concept of intrinsic and extrinsic motivation takes on greater importance. (p. 112)

Of note also in the Educational Psychologist's report was her recommendation that Gita needed to acquire strategies to improve her 'working memory'.

Whitebread (2012: 98–9) has proposed that 'working memory' has three distinctive features: *rehearsal*, *multi-sensory representations* and *limited capacity*. Because capacity for storing information in 'working memory' is limited and decays rapidly after some 30 seconds, another means of holding information for longer is required. By rehearsing information in 'working memory' it is possible to hold it for longer as this allows for the transfer of information to 'long-term memory' where it will be stored for longer, even months and years. Children develop their capacity for rehearsal at an early age, which they then expand throughout primary school. The second feature proposed by Whitebread, *multi-sensory representations*, allows for the storing and manipulation of information as visual images in 'working memory', which strengthens the memory traces in the brain; this is important for children with dyslexia who like Gita struggle to retain sensory information in 'working memory' long enough and in ways that allow for it to be transferred to long-term memory.

Using different senses in unison with one another as with multisensory learning, which was recommended by Gita's Educational Psychologist, is a very powerful way for improving the memory capacity of children with dyslexia and improving their learning. With Whitebread's third feature, *limited capacity*, most adults can hold around seven bits of information in working memory, and as new bits of information enter 'working memory' other bits already stored in the memory are pushed out. Young children such as Gita have less storage than adults and are able to hold fewer bits or items of information in short-term storage, which presents them with challenges in their acquisition of single word recognition and spelling, which is at the root of Gita's difficulties with literacy.

Pradeep

Pradeep is typical of many children whose dyspraxia fails to be identified in early childhood, leading quite often to miscalculations of their abilities and potential by teachers; this is in addition to developing ineffective strategies for learning that then affect their progress. Pradeep's condition is not rare; indeed, the Dyspraxia Foundation suggests that this condition affects up to ten per cent of the general population, with two per cent being affected severely and with males being more affected than females. The extent to which dyspraxia continues to be misunderstood has been reflected by Boon (2010), who commented on how, 'If you ask different professionals what dyspraxia is, you get different answers, depending on their field of expertise…'. Boon went on to indicate how the Dyspraxia Association had defined this condition as '…an impairment or immaturity of the organisation of movement. Associated with this there may be problems of language, perception and thought' (p. 7). We can speculate then that in Pradeep's case it is likely he has experienced impairment and/or immaturity in his organisation of movement, with associated problems of language and thinking, which most probably have been affecting his abilities with planning and elements of his general learning across the curriculum.

Drawing again on neuroscience, we know that as children grow their brains develop, and with this comes the basis for their learning. Neuroscience has also informed us about how every part of our body is connected to our brains, with some parts having many more neurons than others, and some parts of our body being more sensitive and more receptive to stimuli such as touch and pain. In children like Pradeep who have the condition dyspraxia, development is characterised by immaturity, which explains why Pradeep is seen by his teachers to be immature, disorganised and clumsy, and quick to become extremely frustrated and angry when he is struggling to complete practical tasks such as building with blocks.

From a very young age, children with dyspraxia, as in the case of Pradeep, often face greater challenges with everyday activities such as getting themselves dressed, using knives, forks and spoons when eating, climbing stairs and balancing. Some physical activities such as throwing and catching when playing games can also present significant challenges. Students who begin working in Early Years settings quickly realise that movement is involved in almost all outdoor activities where children are encouraged to run and jump, in addition to indoor activities such as drawing and writing that involve physical movement, and of course speaking and singing when they physically use the muscles in their mouths and throats. When muscles in a young child's mouth or throat are affected then speech and even general language processing can become compromised, with the result that children can experience difficulties with articulating words and phrases and ideas as these arise in their thoughts, rendering their speech at times difficult to understand (Macintyre, 2002).

Activity

Take time to access the following: 'Early years experts weigh up the revised ELGs', available at: www.nurseryworld.co.uk/news/article/early-years-experts-weigh-up-the-revised-elgs (accessed: 21 April 2020), which offers responses to proposed changes to Early Learning Goals (ELGs) for the end of the Reception year, which have been piloted in 25 schools in England. Then, consider your own responses to those of the experts.

Referring again to neuroscience, we know that the brain consists of many millions of nerve cells that facilitate learning and, as Macintyre and McVitty (2004: 5–6) have proposed:

> ...work together to receive, analyse and act on information from both external, i.e. environmental sources, and internal feelings, i.e. pain, hunger and the different emotions. As different experiences occur, these neurons join into networks that work

together as systems to facilitate specific functions such as vision or hearing, movement or paying attention… the 'majority of the maturation has occurred by the age of three to four years' (Winkley, 2003).

Movement is also very important in the development of self-esteem. Children with dyspraxia, as in Pradeep's case, may on occasions encounter an unwillingness on the part of their peers to choose them for games. They may have struggled to ride two-wheeled bicycles without stabilisers and later on in school may display very poor handwriting and untidy presentation of written work, accompanied by significant problems with organisation and difficulties learning to tell the time, all of which can result in a lowering of self-esteem and self-efficacy, evidenced by a lessening of motivation. They may also be very easily distracted by others around them, by noise or visual stimuli in their environment or even by their own thoughts, meaning that they may often fail to complete work assignments within given time limits. They may also experience difficulties with sitting still for even short periods of time and can frequently be checked by their teacher for moving too much and 'squirming' in their seats. Physical education (PE) and games lessons may present significant challenges as immaturities in motor coordination mean they struggle to keep up with others when, for example, playing ball games that require them to throw and catch with accuracy, and run and maintain ball control, such as in rounders, soccer, netball or cricket.

Discussion Point

How might staff working with Pradeep adapt his learning environment to promote more physical activity, and should this be their responsibility?

Case Study 10.2: Wellbeing and Obesity

Oscar is nearing completion of Key Stage 1 and whilst his progress in literacy and numeracy have been good, he is experiencing significant difficulties because he is overweight. Since his time in pre-school Oscar has been over-indulged by his parents and has become used to eating a diet that is excessively rich in sugar and carbohydrates. He now struggles to run and is often teased by his peers who frequently exclude him from their games. Oscar's teachers have been very concerned about his being overweight and poor diet and have shared their concerns with his parents, who have appeared resentful of this and tell the teachers that they see nothing wrong in giving Oscar the sort of food that he likes eating; both of Oscar's parents are themselves overweight.

Being active supports effective learning

Signposts to Theory

We know that increasing numbers of children like Oscar are overeating or eating food that is potentially harmful to them and that their levels of nutrition are a rising concern amongst medical professionals. Across the globe, obesity is emerging as a significant problem. The World Health Organization (WHO, 2015) reported on how the number of overweight children under the age of five had increased from 32 million globally in 1990 to 42 million in 2013. The WHO estimated that if this trend continued the number of overweight or obese infants and young children across the globe would rise to some 70 million by 2025. The Health and Social Care Information Centre reported in 2015 that across England the number of children aged 4–5 years in their Reception year in 2013/14 who were obese amounted to 9.5 per cent. Such findings are concerning. Being obese often leads to general health problems, as well as issues of a psychological nature, linked to bullying and teasing, and issues with learning.

Drawing on Erikson's theory we see that Oscar is at the *industry versus inferiority* stage, when winning the approval of his peers is very important, as is developing a sense of pride in his achievements and who he is becoming as a person. Given his obesity and the fact that he struggles to perform well in physical activities, he is likely to encounter some social problems as he moves through this stage. Successful progression, as Erikson proposed, leads to children acquiring a stronger sense of being industrious, coupled with a growth in self-confidence; for Oscar, unsuccessful progression may well lead to subsequent feelings of inferiority and self-doubt – as was also the case with Robbie in Case Study 10.1, though for different reasons.

> ### Critical Question
>
> How might Early Years practitioners and teachers in primary schools work with parents who refuse to accept that their children may experience health problems in later years because of their poor diets?

We know from *behaviourist* theory that feelings of inferiority and self-doubt are likely to become more ingrained as difficulties with running and participating in some physical activities are reinforced by comments from other children. It is likely that Oscar will receive more negative comments during unstructured time when, for example, he is outside of the classroom, during break times and at the beginning and end of the school day. In some respects, he may even feel that he is being bullied, and such feelings may well lead him to become isolated, which, as we saw when exploring the work of Bandura in Chapter 3, will impact negatively on his social learning. Oscar's emotional intelligence may also be impacted upon, as he may at times feel engulfed by feelings arising out of teasing from other children for which he has no immediate solution. We can recall the importance of emotional intelligence on wider learning and how Oscar's intellectual development may be adversely affected by continuing feelings of low self-worth.

> ### Chapter Link
>
> Revisit Chapter 2 and the work of Salovey and Mayer on key factors in emotional intelligence.

The work of Bilton discussed in Chapter 4 is also relevant here when one considers the potential that outdoor learning can offer Oscar. We can also consider the impact of obesity on Oscar's development in terms of his happiness and wellbeing, as discussed in Chapter 2, and how important it is for adults working with Oscar to monitor these aspects of his emotional learning and how they are impacting on his self-efficacy and learning.

> ### Chapter Link
>
> Revisit the ideas of those who have advocated for children's healthy living and the artificial barriers that can impact on children's progress in Chapters 1–5.

Activity

Take the time to look through the British Nutrition Foundation website, available at: www.nutrition.org.uk/ (accessed: 3 October 2020), and then prioritise ten factors that you consider important for good nutrition in the Early Years.

Extended Reading

Fabian, H. and Mould, C. (2009) *Development and Learning for Very Young Children*. London: Sage. A useful resource that focuses on children from 0 to 3 years of age and covers much material, including stages of child development, development and learning, and policy and practice.

Haines, S. J., Summers, J. A., Turnbull, A. P., Turnbull, H. R. and Palmer, S. (2015) 'Fostering Habib's engagement and self-regulation: a case study of a child from a refugee family at home and preschool', *Topics in Early Childhood Special Education*, 35 (1): 28–39. An interesting case study of a child from a refugee family in pre-school, which illustrates cultural differences.

National Children's Bureau, Early Childhood Unit (NCB) (2015) *The Integrated Review: Bringing Together Health and Early Education Reviews at Age Two to Two-and-a-Half*. London: NCB. An excellent insight into assessment at age two and the involvement of different agencies working collaboratively.

SOME CONCLUDING THOUGHTS

The primary aim of this text has been that of supporting students and early career professionals in the field of Early Years and Primary teaching with demonstrating and applying their knowledge and understanding of early childhood from 0 to 7 years of age. These are changing times and there has been a growing realisation of the importance of understanding children's learning and the impact that social and emotional factors can have in early childhood; this has of course been accentuated by the current COVID-19 pandemic. Early Years practitioners and teachers have been challenged to explore new ways of supporting learning in early childhood and to recognise the importance of issues such as emotional health and wellbeing, social learning, and nutrition.

At the same time as practitioners and teachers are responding to the challenges of COVID-19, changes are being introduced by the UK government regarding the Early Years Foundation Stage. Readers can familiarise themselves with these changes, which have just been finalised and which become statutory in September 2020, by accessing the following websites:

Early Years Foundation Stage Reforms Government Consultation:

https://consult.education.gov.uk/early-years-quality-outcomes/early-years-foundation-stage-reforms/supporting_documents/EYFS%20reforms%20consultation.pdf (accessed: 27 July 2020).

Early Years Alliance – 'Changes to the EYFS 2021':

www.eyalliance.org.uk/changes-eyfs-2021 (accessed: 27 July 2020).

It can be emphasised with certainty that young children will now more than ever need the support of informed practitioners and teachers in their learning as they move through the next years.

REFERENCES

Allott, K. and Waugh, D. (2019) 'Talk and communication: couldn't they just sit down and shut up', in C. Carden (ed.), *Primary Teaching*. London: Sage.

Association of Teachers and Lecturers (ATL) (2005) *An Intelligent Look at Emotional Intelligence*. London: ATL.

Attwood, T. (1993) *Asperger's Syndrome: A Guide for Parents and Professionals*. London: Jessica Kingsley.

Attwood, T. (2007) *The Complete Guide to Asperger's Syndrome*. London: Jessica Kingsley.

Aubrey, K. and Riley, A. (2017) *Understanding & Using Challenging Educational Theories*. London: Sage.

Bandura, A. (1977) *Social Learning Theory*. Englewood Cliffs, NJ: Prentice Hall.

Bandura, A. (1997) *Self-Efficacy: The Exercise of Control*. New York: Freeman.

Bilton, H. and Waters, J. (2016) 'Why take young children outside? A critical consideration of the professed aims for outdoor learning in the early years by teachers from England and Wales', *Social Sciences*, 6 (1). doi: https://doi.org/10.3390/socsci6010001.

Boon, M. (2010) *Understanding Dyspraxia: A Guide for Parents and Teachers* (2nd edn). London: Jessica Kingsley.

Bowlby, J. (1988) *A Secure Base: Clinical Applications of Attachment Theory*. London: Routledge.

British Dyslexia Association (BDA) (2012) *Dyscalculia, Dyslexia and Maths*. Available at: www.bdadyslexia.org.uk/dyslexia/neurodiversity-and-co-occurring-differences/dyscalculia-and-maths-difficulties (accessed: October 2020).

Bronfenbrenner, U. (1979) *The Ecology of Human Development*. Cambridge, MA: Harvard University Press.

Bronfenbrenner, U. and Ceci, S. J. (1994) 'Nature–nurture reconceptualized in the developmental perspective: A bioecological model', *Psychological Review*, 101: 568–86.

Brooks, V., Abbott, I. and Bills, L. (2004) *Preparing to Teach in Secondary Schools*. Maidenhead: Open University Press.

Brown, G. (1977) *Child Development*. Shepton Mallet: Open Books.

Brown, S. and Vaughan, C. (2009) *Play: How it Shapes the Brain, Opens the Imagination and Invigorates the Soul*. New York: Avery Penguin Group.

Bruner, J. S. (1960) *The Process of Education*. Cambridge, MA: Harvard University Press.

Bruner, J. S. (1975) 'The ontogenesis of speech acts', *Journal of Child Language*, 2: 1–19.

Bruner, J. S. (1983) *Child's Talk: Learning to Use Language*. New York: Norton.
Buckler, S. and Castle, P. (2014) *Psychology for Teachers*. London: Sage.
Burden, R. (1987) 'Feuerstein's instrumental enrichment programme: important issues in research and evaluation', *European Journal of Psychology of Education*, 2 (1): 3–16.
Campione, J. C. (1989) 'Assisted assessment: a taxonomy of approaches and an outline of strengths and weaknesses', *Journal of Learning Disabilities*, 22 (3): 151–65.
Carr, M. and Lee, W. (2019) *Learning Stories in Practice*. London: Sage.
Children and Young People's Mental Health Coalition (CYPMHC) (2012) *Resilience and Results: How to Improve the Emotional and Mental Well-being of Children and Young People in Your School*. London: CYPMHC.
ChildWise (2015) *The Monitor Pre-School Report: Key Behaviour Patterns Among 0–4 Year Olds*. London: ChildWise.
Chomsky, N. (1965) *Aspects of the Theory of Syntax*. Cambridge: MA: MIT Press.
Colverd, S. and Hodgkin, B. (2011) *Developing Emotional Intelligence in the Primary School*. London: Routledge.
Corsaro, W. A. (1992) 'Interpretative reproduction in children's peer cultures', *Social Psychology Quarterly*, 55 (2): 160–77.
Crombie, M. and Reid, G. (2009) 'The role of early identification models from research and practice', in G. Reid (ed.), *The Routledge Companion to Dyslexia*. New York: Routledge.
Cullis, A. and Hansen, K. (2009) Child Development in the First Three Sweeps of the Millenium Cohort Study, DCSF Research Report RW-007. London: DCSF.
Curran, A. (2012) 'Autism and the brain's working: how far have we got?', *Debate*, 144: 5–6. Leicester: The British Psychological Society.
Daniels, D.H. and Shumow, L. (2002) 'Child development and classroom teaching: a review of the literature and implications for educating teachers', *Applied Developmental Psychology*, 23: 495–526.
Drysdale, J. (2009) 'Overcoming the barriers to literacy: an integrated, contextual workshop approach', in G. Reid (ed.), *The Routledge Companion to Dyslexia*. New York: Routledge.
Erikson, E. (1950) *Childhood and Society*. Harmondsworth: Pelican.
Everatt, J. and Reid, G. (2009) 'Dyslexia: an overview of recent research', in G. Reid (ed.), *The Routledge Companion to Dyslexia*. New York: Routledge.
Feuerstein, R., Rand, Y., Hoffman, M. and Miller, R. (1980) *Instrumental Enrichment*. Baltimore: University Park Press.
Field, F. (2010) *The Foundation Years: Preventing Poor Children Becoming Poor Adults – Report of the Independent Review on Poverty and Life Chances*. London: Cabinet Office.
Fiske, S. T. and Taylor, S. E. (1991) *Social Cognition* (2nd edn). New York: McGraw-Hill.
Fontana, D. (1995) *Psychology for Teachers* (3rd edn). Basingstoke: MacMillan Press.
Frederickson, N. and Cline, T. (2002) *Special Educational Needs, Inclusion and Diversity*. Maidenhead: Open University Press.
Froebel, F. (1887) *The Education of Man* (Translated by Hailmann, W. N.). New York: D. Appleton Century.
Gardner, H. (1983) *Frames of Mind*. London: Fontana.
Ginsberg, K. R., the Committee on Communications and the Committee on Psychosocial Aspects of Child and Family Health (2007) 'The importance of play in promoting healthy child development and maintaining strong parent-child bonds', *Pediatrics*, 119 (1): 182–91.
Goodman, R. (2013) *How to be a Victorian*. London: Penguin Books.
Goleman, D. (1996) *Emotional Intelligence: Why It Can Matter More Than IQ*. London: Bloomsbury.

Gopnik, A. (2009) *The Philosophical Baby: What Children's Minds Tell Us about Truth, Love and the Meaning of Life*. London: Bodley Head.
Gopnik, A. (2012) 'Scientific thinking in young children: Theoretical advances, empirical research and policy implications', *Science*, 28 (337): 1623–7.
Gopnik, A., Meltzoff, A. and Kuhl, P. (2001) *How Babies Think: The Science of Childhood*. London: Phoenix.
Gray, C. and MacBlain, S. F. (2015) *Learning Theories in Childhood* (2nd edn). London: Sage.
Gross, R. D. (1992) *Psychology: The Science of Mind and Behaviour* (2nd edn). London: Hodder & Stoughton.
Hadow Report (1931) *The Primary School*. Available at: https://webarchive.nationalarchives.gov.uk/20101007105102/http://www.ttrb.ac.uk//viewArticle2.aspx?contentId=15840 (accessed: 3 October 2020).
Harlow, H. (1964) 'Early social deprivation and later behavior in the monkey', in A. Abrams, H. H. Gurner and J. E. P. Tomal (eds), *Unfinished Tasks in the Behavioral Sciences*. Baltimore, MD: Williams & Wilkins.
Hayes, N. (1994) *Foundations of Psychology: An Introductory Text*. London: Routledge.
Head, C. (2016) 'Communication and language', in I. Palaiologou (ed.), *The Early Years Foundation Stage: Theory and Practice* (3rd edn). London: Sage.
Heider, R. (1958) *The Psychology of Interpersonal Relations*. New York: Wiley.
Herbert, M. (2005) *Developmental Problems of Childhood and Adolescence: Prevention, Treatment and Training*. Oxford: Blackwell.
Hicks, D. (2004) 'The global dimension in the curriculum', in S. Ward (ed.), *Education Studies: A Student's Guide*. London: RoutledgeFalmer.
Higgs, L. G. (2013) *Theory in Educational Research and Practice in Teacher Education*. Available at: https://files.eric.ed.gov/fulltext/ED567134.pdf (accessed: 8 July 2020).
HM Government (2011) *A New Approach to Child Poverty: Tackling the Causes of Disadvantage and Transforming Families*. Norwich: The Stationery Office.
Holzman, L. (2006) 'Activating postmodernism', *Theory and Psychology*, 16 (1): 109–23.
Hope, S. (2018) 'Principled professionalism in the classroom', in I. Luke and J. Gourd (eds), *Thriving as a Professional Teacher*. London: Routledge.
Horn, P. (1997) *The Victorian Child*. Stroud: Sutton.
Hutchinson, R. (2017) *The Butcher, The Baker, The Candlestick Maker: The Story of Britain through its Census, since 1801*. London: Abacus.
infed.org (2018) *Caring in Education*. Available at: http://infed.org/mobi/caring-in-education/ (accessed: 16 October 2018).
International Labour Organisation (ILO) (2015) *World Report on Child Labour: Paving the Way to Decent Work for Young People*. Geneva: ILO.
IOE (2014) Millennium Cohort Study: Initial findings from the age 11 survey. Available at: www.cls.ioe.ac.uk/page.aspx?&sitesectionid=1330&sitesectiontitle=MCS+age+11+initial+findings
Jarvis, M. (2005) *The Psychology of Effective Learning and Teaching*. Cheltenham: Nelson Thornes Ltd.
Jones, M. (2016) *Talking and Learning with Young Children*. London: Sage.
Kelley, H. H. (1967) 'Attribution theory in social psychology', in D. Levine (ed.), *Nebraska Symposium on Motivation* (Vol. 15). Lincoln, NE: University of Nebraska Press.
Knowles, G. and Holmström (2013) *Understanding Family Diversity and Home-School Relations: A Guide for Students and Practitioners in Early Years and Primary Settings*. London: Routledge.
Kucirkova, N. and Sakr, M. (2015) 'Child-father creative text-making at home with crayons, iPad collage and PC', *Thinking Skills and Creativity*, 17: 59–73.

Laevers, F. (ed.) (2005) *Well-Being and Involvement in Care Settings: A Process-Oriented Self-Evaluation Instrument*. Leuven, Belgium: Research Centre for Experiential Learning, Leuven University.

Lawson, W. (2013) 'Remembering school', in M. Prior (ed.), *Learning and Behavior Problems in Asperger Syndrome*. New York: The Guilford Press.

Linden, J. (2005) *Understanding Child Development: Linking Theory to Practice*. London: Hodder Education.

Luke, I., MacBlain, S. F. and Golder, G. (2020) 'Children, young people and education', in S. Capel and R. Blair (2020) (eds), *Debates in Physical Education*. London: Routledge.

MacBlain, S. F. (2014) *How Children Learn*. London: Sage.

MacBlain, S. F., Long, L. and Dunn, J. (2015) *Dyslexia, Literacy and Inclusion: Child-Centred Perspectives*. London: Sage.

MacBlain, S. F. (2018) *Learning Theories for Early Years Practice*. London: Sage.

MacBlain, S. F. (2020) *Child Development for Teachers*. London: Sage.

MacBlain, S. F. and Gray, C. (2016) 'Understanding Bandura', *Early Years Educator*, May.

MacBlain, S. F., Dunn, J. and Luke, I. (2017) *Contemporary Childhood*. London: Sage.

Macintyre, C. (2002) *Play for Children with Special Needs: Including Children Aged 3–8*. London: David Fulton.

Macintyre, C. and McVitty, K. (2004) *Movement and Learning in the Early Years: Supporting Dyspraxia (DCD) and Other Difficulties*. London: Paul Chapman.

Main, M. and Solomon, J. (1986) 'Discovery of insecure-disorganized/disorientated attachment patterns: procedures, findings and implications for the classification of behaviour', in T. B. Brazelton and M. Yogman (eds), *Affective Development in Infancy*. Norwood, NJ: Ablex.

Malaguzzi, L. (1998) *The Hundred Languages of Children*. Norwood, NJ: Ablex.

Mayes, S. D. and Calhoun, S. L. (2003) 'Relationship between Asperger Syndrome and high-functioning autism', in M. Prior (ed.), *Learning and Behaviour Problems in Asperger Syndrome*. New York: Guilford Press.

Maynard, T. and Waters, J. (2007) 'Learning in the outdoor environment: A missed opportunity?', *Early Years*, 27: 255–65.

McKee, B. (2004) *'Child protection in education: training the trainers'*. Paper presented at European CAPE conference, 10–12 July, Lancaster, UK.

McLeod, S. A. (2012) *Attribution Theory*. Available at: www.simplypsychology.org/attribution-theory.html (accessed: 2 March 2020).

McMillan, D. (2009) 'Preparing for educare: student perspectives on early years training in Northern Ireland', *International Journal of Early Years Education*, 17 (3): 219–35.

Mercer, J. (2018) *Child Development: Concepts and Theories*. London: Sage.

Miller, L. and Pound, L. (2011) *Theories and Approaches to Learning in the Early Years*. London: Sage.

Moyles, J. (1989) *Just Playing? The Role and Status of Play in Early Childhood Education*. Milton Keynes: Open University Press.

NAHT (2018) *NAHT Rejects Bold Beginnings Approach to Early Years Learning*. Available at: www.naht.org.uk/news-and-opinion/news/curriculum-and-assessment-news/naht-rejects-bold-beginnings-approach-to-early-years-learning/ (accessed: 16 May 2020).

Neumann, M. and Neumann, D. (2014) 'Touch screen tablets and emergent literacy', *Early Childhood Education Journal*, 42: 231–9.

Nuffield Foundation (2009) 'English and Romanian adoptee study: English-Romanian adoption'. Available at: www.nuffieldfoundation.org/project/english-and-romanian-adoptee-study (accessed: 3 October 2020).

Nutbrown, C. (2006) *Threads of Thinking: Young Children Learning and the Role of Early Education*. London: Sage.

Nutbrown, C. and Clough, P. (2014) *Early Childhood Education, History, Philosophy and Experience* (2nd edn). London: Sage.

Ofsted (2017) *Bold Beginnings: The Reception Curriculum in a Sample of Good and Outstanding Primary Schools*. Manchester: Office for Standards in Education.

Office for National Statistics (ONS) (2015) *Measuring National Well-Being: Insights into Children's Mental Health and Well-Being*. Available at: www.ons.gov.uk/ ons/rel/ wellbeing/measuring-national-well-being/children-and-young-people-s-well-being-in-the-uk-october-2015/art-insights-into-children-s-mental-healthand-well-being.html (accessed: 3 January 2018).

Palmer, S. (2006) *The Toxic Child*. London: Orion Books.

Papatheodorou, T. and Potts, D. (2016) 'Pedagogy in practice', in I. Palaiologou (ed.), *The Early Years Foundation Stage: Theory and Practice* (3rd edn). London: Sage.

Paton, G. (2012) 'New-style "nappy curriculum" will damage childhood', *The Telegraph*, 6 February. Available at: www.telegraph.co.uk/education/ educationnews/9064870/New-style-nappy-curriculum-will-damage-childhood. html (accessed: 7 August 2019).

Pea, R. D. (1993) 'Practices of distributed intelligence and designs for education', in G. Salomon (ed.), *Distributed Cognitions*. New York: Cambridge University Press.

Pearce, C. (2009) *A Short Introduction to Attachment and Attachment Disorder*. London: Jessica Kingsley.

Piaget, J. P. (1952) *The Origins of Intelligence in Children*. New York: International Universities Press.

Platt, L. (2007) *Poverty and Ethnicity in the UK*. York: Joseph Rowntree Foundation.

Pramling Samuelsson, I. and Asplund Carlsson, M. (2008) 'The playing learning child: towards a pedagogy of early childhood', *Scandinavian Journal of Educational Research*, 52 (6): 623–41.

Pring, R. (2007) *John Dewey: A Philosopher of Education for Our Time?* London: Continuum International Publishing Group.

Reid, G. (ed.) (2009) *The Routledge Companion to Dyslexia*. New York: Routledge.

Reid, G. and Came, F. (2009) 'Identifying and overcoming the barriers to learning in an inclusive context' in G. Reid (ed.), *The Routledge Companion to Dyslexia*. New York: Routledge.

Roffey, S., Jamison, L. and Davis, C. (2016) 'Behaviour', in D. Wyse and S. Rogers (eds), *A Guide to Early Years & Primary Teaching*. London: Sage.

Rogoff, B. (2003) *The Cultural Nature of Human Development*. New York: Oxford University Press.

Rose, J. and Wood, E. (2016) 'Child development', in D. Wyse and S. Rogers (eds), *A Guide to Early Years & Primary Teaching*. London: Sage.

Rose, S. A., Feldman, J. F. and Jankowski, J. J. (2003) 'The building blocks of cognition', *The Journal of Pediatrics*, 143 (4): 54–61.

Rousseau, J. J. (1762/1911) *Emile*. London: J. M. Dent.

Rutter, M. (1981) *Maternal Deprivation Reassessed* (2nd edn). Harmondsworth: Penguin Books.

Salovey, P. and Mayer, J.D. (1990) 'Emotional intelligence', *Imagination, Cognition and Personality*, 9(3): 185–211.

Schaffer, H. R. and Emerson, P. E. (1964) 'The development of social attachments in infancy', *Monographs of the Society for Research in Child Development*, 29 (94): 1–77.

Schaler, J. A. (ed.) (2006) *Howard Gardner Under Fire: The Rebel Psychologist Faces His Critics*. Chicago, IL: Carus Publishing Company.

Silber, K. (1965) *Pestalozzi: The Man and His Work*. London: Routledge & Kegan Paul.

Skinner, B. (1953) *Science and Human Behaviour*. New York: Macmillan.

Skinner, B. (1957) *Verbal Behaviour*. New York: Appleton-Century-Crofts.
Smidt, S. (2011) *Introducing Bruner: A Guide for Practitioners and Students in Early Years Education*. London: Routledge.
Smith, K. S., Cowie, H. and Blades, M. (2003) *Understanding Children's Development* (4th edn). Oxford: Blackwell.
Smith, M. K. (2002/2008) 'Howard Gardner and multiple intelligences', in *The Encyclopedia of Informal Education*. Available at: www.infed.org/thinkers/gardner.htm (accessed: 3 October 2020).
Teichert, L. and Anderson, A. (2014) 'I don't even know what blogging is: the role of digital media in a five-year-old girl's life', *Early Child Development and Care*, 184 (11): 1677–91.
The Compass School (2019) *What is Provocation?* Available at: www.thecompassschool.com/blog/what-is-provocation/ (accessed: 26 November 2019).
Tizard, B. and Hughes, M. (1984) *Young Children Learning: Learning and Thinking at Home and at School*. London: Fontana.
Vygotsky, L. S. (1978) *Mind in Society: The Development of Higher Psychological Processes*. Cambridge, MA: Harvard University Press.
Vygotsky, L. S. (1987–1998) *The Collected Works of L. S. Vygotsky. Volume I: Problems of General Psychology. Volume II: The Fundamentals of Defectology. Volume III: Problems of the Theory and History of Psychology. Volume IV: The History of Development of Higher Mental Functions. Volume V: Child Psychology* (Editor of the English translation: R. W. Rieber). New York: Plenum Press.
Walsh, G. (2017) 'Why playful teaching and learning?', in G. Walsh, D. McMillan and C. McGuinness (eds), *Playful Teaching and Learning*. London: Sage.
Walsh, G. (2018) 'Foreword', in S. MacBlain, *Learning Theories for Early Years Practice*. London: Sage.
Walsh, G. (2019) 'Towards playful teaching and learning in practice', in A. Andreassen-Becher, E. Bjørnestad and H. Dehnæs-Hogsnes (eds), *Lek I Begynneropplæringen*. Oslo: Universitetsforlaget.
Walsh, G. and Gillespie, S. (2020) *Life after Lockdown in the Early Years Classroom: Embracing Challenges as Opportunities*. Available at: www.stran.ac.uk/life-after-lockdown-in-the-early-years-classroom-embracing-challenges-as-opportunities/ (accessed: 9 July 2020).
Watson, J. B. (1928) *Psychological Care of Infant and Child*. New York: Norton.
Wells, G. (1990) *The Meaning Makers: Children Learning Language and Using Language to Learn*. London: Hodder & Stoughton.
Wertsch, J. V. (ed.) (1981) *The Concept of Activity in Soviet Psychology*. Armonk, NY: M. E. Sharpe.
Wheldall, K. (2012) *The Behaviourist in the Classroom*. Oxford: Routledge.
Whitebread, D. (2012) *Developmental Psychology & Early Childhood Education*. London: Sage.
Willett, R. J. (2015) 'The discursive construction of "good parenting" and digital media: the case of children's virtual world games', *Media, Culture and Society*, 37 (7): 1060–75.
Wilshaw, M. (2014) *Unsure Start: HCMI's Early Years Annual Report 2012/13 Speech 2014*.
Wood, D., Bruner, J.S. and Ross, G. (1976) 'The role of tutoring in problem solving', *Journal of Child Psychology and Psychiatry*, 17 (2): 81–100.
Wood, E. (2008) *The Routledge Reader in Early Childhood Education*. London: Routledge.
World Health Organization (WHO) (2015) *Facts and Figures on Childhood Obesity*. Available at: www.who.int/end-childhood-obesity/facts/en/ (accessed: 30 October 2015).

INDEX

accommodation 60, 61
adult-supported learning 33, 47–8, 92, 102, 112
  see also scaffolding
affective processes, and self-efficacy 32, 33f, 102t, 103
Ainsworth, Mary 35, 98, 109
anal stage 13, 27
  key features 106t
  successful/unsuccessful progression 107, 107t
antisocial behaviour 37, 43
artificial barriers, challenging 78–9
Asperger's syndrome
  case study 9.2 124–7
assessment 79
  case study 8.2 110–14
  of happiness and wellbeing 36–7
  and observation 16, 111–12
  of specific learning difficulties 55, 124, 130–1, 135
assimilation 60, 61
Astoria, Waldorf 16
attachment 34–8
  behaviourist approach 34, 110
  classifications 35
  evolutionary approach 34–5, 110
  stages 38
attachment disorder 34, 35
  case studies 7.1, 8.1 (Robbie) 97, 106, 108, 109–10
attention 20, 47, 48
attribution theory 113–14
Attwood, T. 124–5
Aubrey, K. 64
autism/autistic spectrum 37, 55
  see also Asperger's Syndrome

autonomy versus shame stage 29
  key features 106t
  successful/unsuccessful progression 107t, 108

BAME communities 44–5
Bandura, Albert
  psychological processes and self-efficacy 32, 33f, 102t, 102–3
  social learning theory 32–3, 45–6, 90, 92, 99, 101–3, 113, 140
banking method 64–5
behaviour modeling 45
behaviour modification 56, 101, 103
Behaviour Support Service 130
behaviourism 17, 90, 91, 92, 112
  and attachment 34, 110
  case study 7.2 100–1, 103–4
  emergence 19–20
  and emotional learning 99, 102, 140
  and empiricism 11
  and language development 52–3, 119t
  and play vs. exploration 67
  relevance today 19–20, 56
  and social learning 56
  sociocultural theory compared 19
Bilton, Helen 70–1, 140
Bold Beginnings (Ofsted) 66
Boon, M. 136
Bowlby, John 34–5, 37, 98
brain development 80–1, 137
  and Asperger's Syndrome 124–5
brainstem 80
bridging 47–8, 108–9
Bristol Language Development Project 120

Bronfenbrenner, Urie
    ecological systems model 48–9, 48f, 99, 126
    and Head Start 77
Brown, G. 62, 64, 103
Bruner, Jerome 20, 62–3, 90, 112, 113
    modes of representation 62–3, 102–3
    scaffolding 63, 92, 113, 122–3
Buckler, S. 20
bullying 44, 139, 140
    see also cyberbullying

Calhoun, S. L. 124
Came, F. 135
care, ethics of 55–6, 114
Carlsson, Asplund 67
Carr, M. 81, 83
Castle, P. 20
cerebral cortex 80
child, recognising the concept of 9–21
child-centred approaches 20, 26, 71
child labour 7
Child Psychologists 42
child's perspective on learning 69
childhood
    differences in 42f
    emergence 10–12
Children and Young People's Mental Health Coalition (CYPMHC) 133–4
ChildWise 81
cholera 16
Chomsky, Noam
    and the behaviourist tradition 52–3
    and language development 52–3, 119t
chronosystem 48f, 49, 99
classical conditioning 34, 110
Claxton, G. 27
Cline, T. 79, 111
Clough, P. 66
cognitive development and learning 2, 35, 59–72, 90, 102, 122
    and emotional intelligence 29, 132
    innate foundations 47
    and language development 54, 119
    and love 99
    and neuroscience 80
cognitive perspective 20
cognitive processes, and self-efficacy 32, 33f, 102f, 102–3
cognitive psychology 20
cognitive structure, and mediated learning 79
Colverd, S. 32
communication
    in Te Whāriki 75, 76t
    see also language and learning

communities and societies
    Bronfenbrenner on 48
    COVID-19 effects 2, 42
    Rogoff on 49–50, 90, 126–7, 133
    Rousseau on 11–12
    in Te Whāriki 75, 76t
    Vygotsky on 47, 54, 62, 119t
community development 77–8
The Compass School 90
compulsory school attendance 15
concepts
    and Asperger's Syndrome 125–6
    schema compared 60
concrete operational stage 61, 109
conduct disorder 133–4
conservation 61
constructivism 20, 60
Coronavirus (COVID-19) 1, 2, 10, 29, 31, 42, 43, 78, 82, 83, 143
covariation model 113–14
creativity and creative thinking 17, 74, 90, 119, 130
critical pedagogy 65
Crombie M. 134
Cullis, A. 43–4
cultural norms 62
cultural tools 46–7, 108, 122
culture
    and language development 122
    Vygotsky on 46–7, 108
Curran, A. 98
curriculum
    Ofsted review of Reception year 4–5
    return to formal 64
    target-driven, vs social and emotional needs 56
cyber bullying 83

Daniels, D. H. 19–20
decentring 61
'descriptions' of learning 2
developmental readiness 4–5
    Reception 4–5
    Year 1 5
    Year 2 5
Dewey, John 17–18, 90
dialogue 65, 112, 113
diet and nutrition 133, 138, 139
digital learning 81–3
disabilities
    and bridging 48
    and poverty 45
    and scaffolding 63
    see also Asperger's Syndrome; dyslexia; dyspraxia; learning difficulties; special educational needs

disadvantaged families 77–8
disorganised attachment 35
diversity, and poverty 44–5
Drysdale, J. 135
dynamic assessment 78, 79, 111–12
dysfunctional parents and families 26, 43
    case studies 7.1, 8.1, 9.1, 10. 1 (Robbie) 96, 97–8, 99, 108, 109–10, 121–2, 123, 132–3
dyslexia 55
    case studies 9.1, 10.1 (Gita) 119, 134–6
dyspraxia 55
    case studies 8.1, 9.1, 10. 1 (Pradeep) 106, 118–19, 130, 136–8

Early Years Alliance – 'Change to the EYFS 2021' 143
Early Years Foundation Stage Reforms Government Consultation 143
ecological systems model (bioecological model) 48–9, 48f, 99, 126
ecological theories 20
Educational Psychology/Psychologists 1, 55, 70, 118
    assessments and recommendations by 124, 130–1, 135–6
egocentrism 43
Emerson, Peggy 37–8, 110
Emile (Rousseau) 11
'emotional apprenticeship' 27
emotional disorder 134
emotional growth, valuing 13
emotional intelligence 29–31, 140
    case study 10.1 (Robbie) 132–3
    key factors in developing 30–1, 132
emotional learning and development 11, 31, 35, 25–39, 95–104, 120, 140
    case study 7.1 96–9
    case study 7.2 100–4
    and love 99
    and neuroscience 80
    and play/outdoor learning 14, 90, 91–2
    vs. targets 56
emotional management styles 31, 133
empathy
    development in children 29, 42, 43, 119, 122
    lack in parents 98
    in teachers 55, 114
empiricism 11, 19
enactive mode 62–3, 103
English Early Years Statutory Framework 71
environment
    exploration of 51, 67, 76t, 90
    importance 2, 17
    interaction and engagement with 12, 13, 31, 60, 69, 90, 91

    interrelation with genetics 81
    see also ecological systems model; outdoor learning
environmental stimuli 19, 79, 138
Erikson, Erik
    stages of development 28–9, 97–8, 108, 119, 122, 131, 132t, 133t, 139–40
evolutionary approach to attachment 34–5, 110
exosystem 48f, 49, 99
experiential learning 18, 46
exploration 74
    environmental 51, 67, 76t, 90
    vs. play 67
expressive language 7, 118, 120
external symbolic stage 54, 121
extra-mainstream practice 73–84

Farr, William 16
Feuerstein, Reuven 78, 92, 102, 112, 113
Field, F. 44
fine motor skills 4, 5
Fiske, S. T. 113
Fontana, D. 2, 43, 60, 90
Forest Schools 70
formal operational stage 61, 109
Foundation Phase Framework for Children's Learning (Wales) 71
Frederickson, N. 79, 111
Freire, Paulo 64–5, 113
Freud, Sigmund 13, 27–8
    stages of development 13, 27–8, 96t, 97, 97t, 107, 119, 131, 132t, 133t
Froebel, Friedrich 14–15

Gardner, Howard 63–4
genetic (inherited) factors 11, 18
    autism and Asperger's Syndrome 37, 125
    interrelation with environment 81
genital stage 13, 28
'gifts' 15
Ginsberg, K. R. 90, 91, 92
Goleman, Daniel 31, 133
Goodman, Ruth 13–14, 28
Gopnik, Alison 50–1
Graham, George 16
Gray, C. 20, 50–1, 54, 121–2

Hadow Report (1931) 15
Hansen, K. 43–4
happiness and wellbeing
    assessing 36–7
    and obesity 140
    and secure attachment 36
    in Te Whāriki 75
    see also health and wellbeing

Harlow, H. 34
Hayes, N. 60
Head, C. 120
Head Start 77
Health and Social Care Information
    Centre 139
health and wellbeing 15, 77, 129–41
    case study 10.1 130–8
    case study 10.2 138–41
    mental 83
Health Visitors 42, 96
hearing difficulties 4
Heider, R. 113
Her Majesty's Chief Inspector (HMCI) 4
Herbert, M. 125
Hicks, D. 10
Hodgkin, B. 32
holistic approaches 26, 76
Holmström, R. 44–5
Holocaust 78
homeless children 15
Hope, S. 26, 56
hormones 80
Horn, P. 15
Hughes, M. 14
'hundred languages of children' 75

iconic mode 62, 63, 103
identification 45
identity versus role confusion stage 29
imitation 16, 45, 101–2, 111, 113
    and language acquisition 52, 53
industry versus inferiority stage 29,
    119, 131
    key features 132t
    successful/unsuccessful progression 132t,
        139–40
initiative versus guilt stage 29, 119, 122
innate ability to learn 47, 48, 62, 74, 108
    language 51, 52
insecure attachment: ambivalent 35, 109
insecure attachment: avoidant 35, 109
instrumental conceptualism 62
instrumental enrichment 78–9
intellectual development 40, 60–5, 92,
    103, 111
    advancing understanding of 16–20
*An Intelligent Look at Emotional
    Intelligence* 27
internalisation of symbolic tools stage
    54, 121–2
International Labour Organisation 7
intuitive stage 61, 102, 119, 131
    features 132t
    successful/unsuccessful progression 132t
invitations vs. provocations 90

involvement, assessing 36–7
Isaacs, Susan 28, 90

Jarvis, M. 2
Jones, M. 52, 122
Joseph, Keith 18

Kelley, H. H. 113
kinaesthetic memory 62
Knowles, G. 44–5

Laboratory School, Chicago 18
Laevers, Freire 36
Language Acquisition Device 52
language and learning 29, 96, 106, 117–27, 131
    behaviourist view 52–3, 92
    and brain development 80
    case study 9.1 118–23
    case study 9.2 124–7
    and dyspraxia 137
    language development stages 54, 121–2
    and play 53, 92, 119
    and social learning 51–5, 90
    and the symbolic mode 63, 103
'language play' 67
latency stage 13, 28, 119, 131
    key features 132t
    successful/unsuccessful progression 132t
Lawson, Wendy 125–6
learning
    assessing 79
    and brain development 80–1
    child's perspective 69
    concept of 2
    digital 81–3
    and nature 12–13
    outdoor 70–1
    and play 13–15, 66–8, 87–93
    teachers as partner in 74–5
    valuing emotional growth in 13
learning difficulties 17, 78
    see also Asperger's Syndrome; dyslexia;
        dyspraxia; special educational needs
Lee, W. 81, 83
Leuven Wellbeing and Involvement
    Scales 36–7
libido (sexual energy) 13, 27, 28, 97, 119, 131
life expectancy, 1840s 16
listening
    by children 17, 53
    to children 28, 113, 120
literacy 4, 5, 82, 130–1, 133, 134, 136, 138
    emotional 30
Little One's nursery 88–9
Locke, John 7, 11, 13, 14, 19
love 28, 98–9

MacBlain S. F. 20, 50–1, 54, 121–2, 135
Macintyre, C. 137–8
macrosystem 48f, 49
Main, M. 35, 109
Malaguzzi, Loris 74–5
Maltings House School 28
'mastery' 33, 102
maternal deprivation 35, 37
mathematics 5, 16, 17, 52, 64, 111, 112
Mayer, John 30–1, 132
Mayes, S. D. 124
Maynard, T. 71
McLeod, S. A. 113–14
McMillan, D. 3
McMillan, Margaret and Rachel 15–16
McVitty, K. 137–8
mediated learning 79, 92, 113
    key features 79
medical inspections in schools 16
memory 17, 20, 47, 48
    see also kinaesthetic memory; working memory
mental health and wellbeing, and social media 83
Mercer, J. 42, 43, 108
mesosystem 48f, 49, 99
microsystem 48f, 49, 99
Millennium Cohort Study 52
Miller, L. 15
modelling
    behaviour 45
    empathy 43
    language structures 121
    learning strategies 111
    symbolic 45
Montessori, Maria 17
    'planes' or 'stages' 17
motivation 45
motivational processes, and self-efficacy 32, 33f, 102f, 103
motor skills 4, 5
Moyles, Janet 69
multiple attachments 37–8, 110
'multiple intelligences' 63–4
multisensory approach 131, 135, 136
music and singing 15, 16, 89
myelination 81

'narrative' approach 17
National Association of Head Teachers (NAHT) 66
nativism 11
nature 12–13, 14, 16 *see also* outdoor learning
negative reinforcement 56, 99
Neumann, D. 82

Neumann, M. 82
neurons 80–1, 137–8
neuroscience 80–1, 135–6, 137
neurotransmitters 80, 81
A New Approach to Child Poverty (UK government report, 2013) 44, 45
nineteenth century childhood 15–16
    see also Victorian era
Noddings, Nel 55–6, 114
non-verbal communication 120
numeracy 4, 133, 138
Nursery Movement 15
Nutbrown, Cathy 60, 66, 68

obesity
    case study 10.2 138–41
observation
    and assessment 16, 111–12
    of behaviours 11, 19
    by children 33, 45, 101–2
    Malaguzzi on 74
    in Steiner-Waldorf schools 17
Office for National Statistics 83
Ofsted curriculum review (2017) 4–5
operant conditioning 34, 91, 99, 101, 103–4, 110, 112
oral stage 13, 27
    key features 96t
    successful/unsuccessful progression 97, 97t
'original sin' 11
outdoor learning 14, 15, 70–1, 75, 140
    case study 6.1 88–92

Palmer, S. 51–2
Papatheodorou, T. 19
parent–child interaction 122–3
Paton, Graeme 66
Pea, R. D. 47
Pearce, C. 98, 109
Pestalozzi, Johann 12–13, 14
phallic stage 13, 27–8
physical activity
    and dyspraxia 118–19, 137, 138
    and the enactive mode 62, 103
    and obesity 139, 140
Piaget, Jean 20, 60–1, 67, 91, 111, 132
    schema 60
    stages of development 60–1, 97, 102, 106t, 107t, 109, 119, 131, 132t, 133t
    Vygotsky compared 19
Platt, L. 44–5
play
    case study 6.1 88–93
    with children of the same gender 131
    vs. exploration 67

and language development 53, 92, 119
as a pedagogic approach 1, 66–8, 87–93
recognising value of 13–15
and self-expression 28
in Te Whāriki 75, 76t
'play spiral' 69
positive reinforcement 20, 56, 91
Potts, D. 19
Pound, L. 15
poverty 37
and disability 45
and diversity 44–5
impact on social learning 43–4
practical intelligence 54
Pramling Samuelsson, Ingrid 67–8
preconceptual stage 61
key features 106t
successful/unsuccessful progression 107t
preoperational stage 60–1, 102, 119, 131
primitive stage 54, 121
Pring, Richard 18
problem-solving 74, 76t
adult-supported 48, 63, 111–12, 113
adults and children compared 51
children's dynamic qualities 62
concrete operational stage 61, 109
and dialogue 65
and language development 54, 103, 121
and play 92
processing speed 130, 131, 135
progressive education 17–18
Provision of School Meals Act (1906) 15
provocations vs. invitations 90
psychoanalysis 27, 28
psychodynamic tradition 13, 27, 97, 98, 107
psychology 2, 13, 27
psychosocial development theory 28–9

questioning 74, 75, 113, 120, 122

Rachel McMillan College 15
reading 4, 16, 17, 44, 82, 111, 119, 130, 131, 135
receptive language 17, 120
Reggio Emilia 74–5, 90, 120
Reid, G. 134, 135
reinforcement 19, 20, 56, 67, 91, 92, 99, 102, 103–4, 112, 140
'relational' care 55, 114
relationships
emotionally impoverished 101
and learning and development 16, 32, 47, 76t, 108, 119
limited opportunities to form 99
and play 92
in Steiner-Waldorf schools 16–17
and trust and mistrust stage 97–8, 97t

repetition 17
Riley, A. 64
Roffey, S. 56
Rogoff, Barbara 49–50, 90, 126–7, 133
role model and modelling 13, 29, 131, 133
poor 26, 27
Romanian Adoptees Study, UK 37
Rose, J. 3–4, 26, 60
Rousseau, Jean-Jacques 7, 11–12, 13, 14
routines, feeding and sleeping 96, 98
Rutter, Michael 37

Salovey, Peter 30–1, 132
Save the Children 52
scaffolding 63, 92, 113, 122–3
Schaffer, Rudolph 37–8, 110
schema 60
concepts compared 60
secure attachment 34, 35, 36, 109
selection processes, and self-efficacy 32, 33f, 102t, 103
self-confidence 29, 65, 92, 98, 101, 111, 108, 112, 139
self-doubt 108, 140
self-efficacy 31–4, 92, 99, 108, 111, 133, 134, 138, 140
case study 7.2 100–4
psychological processes and 32, 33f, 102t, 102–3
self-esteem 32, 92, 98, 99, 101, 102, 108, 125, 134, 138
sensitive periods 17
sensorimotor stage 60, 97
key features 96t
successful/unsuccessful progression 97t
sensory development 4
separation 34
separation difficulties 35
case study 8.1 (Robbie) 106, 109–10
Shumow, L. 19–20
Silber, K. 12
Skinner, B. 56
sleep 133
smallpox vaccinations 16
Smidt, S. 122
'smiley face' stickers 56, 100, 101
Smith, K. S. 2, 67
social change agents 64
social cognitive theory *see* social learning theory
social constructivist theories 20
social constructivist (sociocultural) theory (Vygotsky) 46–8, 54, 92, 120–1
behaviourism compared 19
social context 46, 50, 54, 126–7
social distancing 29, 42, 43
social intelligence 30

social interaction/s 17, 31, 32, 42, 62, 74, 92
social interactionist theory 78, 79
social language 53–5, 90
social learning and development 11, 16, 31, 35, 41–57, 75, 105–15, 140
  and behaviourism 56
  case study 7.1, 99
  case study 8.1 106–10
  case study 8.2 110–14
  impact of poverty 43–5
  and language development 51–5, 121–2
  and love 99
  and neuroscience 80
  and play 14, 90, 92
social learning (social cognitive) theory (Bandura) 32–3, 45–6, 90, 92, 99, 101–3, 113, 140
social media 83
social reform 15–16
societies *see* communities and societies
sociocultural theory *see* social constructivist theory
Solomon, J. 35, 109
special educational needs
  see also Asperger's Syndrome; dyslexia; dyspraxia; learning difficulties
Special Educational Needs (and Disability) Coordinator (SEN(D)Co) 124, 135
Speech and Language Therapy Service 55, 118
'star charts' 20, 56
static assessment 79, 111, 114
Steiner, Rudolf 16–17
Steiner-Waldorf schools 16
strange situation 35
Sure Start 77–8
symbolic mode 62, 63, 103
symbolic modelling 45
synapses 81

tablet computers 81–2
tabula rasa (blank slate) 11
Taylor, S. E. 113
Te Whāriki 75–7
  key goals 76t
  key principles 76t
teachers as co-learners 74–5
Thatcher, Margaret 18

theory, importance of 3–4
'theory consilience' approach 3–4
Tizard, B. 14
toilet training and use 4, 27, 107
trust versus mistrust stage 29
  key features 96t
  successful/unsuccessful progression 97t, 97–8

Victorian era 13–14, 28 '
'virtue' caring 44, 114
visual difficulties 4
visual recognition 47
Vygotsky, Lev
  and adult-supported learning 47–8, 92, 112, 113
  and culture and cultural tools 46–7, 108, 122
  and intellectual development 62
  and language development 53–5, 90, 119t, 120–2
  language development stages 54, 121–2
  Piaget compared 19
  social constructivist (sociocultural) theory 19, 46–8, 54, 92, 120–1
  and social learning 46–8, 92, 120–1
  zone of proximal development 111

Walsh, G. 3
Waters, Jane 70–1
Watson, J. B. 19
wellbeing
  see happiness and wellbeing; health and wellbeing; mental health and wellbeing
Wellbeing and Involvement Scales 36–7
Wells, G. 120
Wertsch, J. V. 47, 108
Whitebread, D. 32, 46, 54, 136
Wilshaw Report (2012/13) 44
Wood, D. 63
Wood, E. 66
Wood, F. 3–4, 26, 60
working memory 130, 131, 135, 136
  limited capacity 136
  multi-sensory representations 136
  rehearsal 136
World Health Organization 139

zone of proximal development 111